ABRAHAM LINCOLN AND THE ACCIDENTAL ANTI-CHRIST

Copyright © 2017 by Prism S. Thomas

All rights reserved

Published by:
G. Stempien Publishing Company
New Quay, Wales UK

Other books about Lincoln by the same author:

*Abraham Lincoln's Grave Robbing: Debunked*
*Abraham Lincoln battles the Antichrist (historical fiction)*

# INTRODUCTION

This is a piece of history of which few people are aware: Napoleon III's battle with Abraham Lincoln. The contest will be for the possession and control of not only the United States of America but ultimately the entire world. And the American Civil War was raging in the midst of this confrontation.

Everyone knows who Abraham Lincoln was: the 16th president of the United States who oversaw the War Between the States and who finally brought an end to slavery in America.

Not as many people are truly familiar with Napoleon III, who during his reign, was known throughout Europe and the East as the true Anti-Christ. Even fewer people are widely knowledgeable about Napoleon III's most powerful ally, Pope Pius IX, and practically no one at all knows of the existence of the mysterious Major Frazer who was the French emperor's advisor and a man who seemed to possess supernatural abilities.

This book is going to examine all of these figures and how they relate to Abraham Lincoln and his long-standing battle with

Napoleon III. In 1864 the French emperor was the most powerful leader in the world and, as noted, was feared by many to be the true Anti-Christ of the Bible. This feature of his background will be highlighted periodically and placed in proper perspective. In fact, the life of Napoleon III had many bizarre and confounding facets to it which made it understandable why so many millions believed he was the Beast of Satan.

At the same time, the life of Lincoln will be placed in comparison with that of Napoleon III, revealing some intriguing similarities. What is to unfold is a history of these two great leaders that has rarely if ever before been documented this extensively.

## ALLIES

One of Louis Napoleon's staunchest allies was Pope Pius IX. A brief look at the pontiff is in order because he is of such significance to the court of Napoleon III. He was born Giovanni Maria Masti-Ferretti on May 13, 1792 at Sinigaglia, Italy, the fourth son of Count Jerome and Countess Catherine Vollazi.

In an odd coincidence it was on May 13, 1917 that the Virgin Mary made her initial appearance at Fatima which is one of the most important of all Marian apparitions. In another peculiar coincidence, it was this pope who declared the Immaculate Conception as a doctrine of the Church many decades **before** the Fatima appearance.

A striking parallel between the pope and Napoleon III is that both men seemed to begin their careers with good intentions and then suddenly - very abruptly - suffered a total change of personality. This change in personality is factual and will be duly documented!

Some might attribute the change to the influence of supernatural forces, but that would be outside the scope of this work. However, it is important to note that because many millions of people accepted Louis Napoleon as being the Anti-Christ their reactions to him were often of a hysterical and exaggerated nature.

The Emperor Napoleon III was born on April 20, 1808. Ironically, Adolf Hitler was also born on April $20^{th}$. The birth of Louis Napoleon - later to become Napoleon III- was a harbinger of great and terrible things to come and bordered on the miraculous itself.

> "On April 20th, (1808) a Wednesday, at one o'clock in
> the morning, at No. 17 of the Rue Lafitte,
> then Rue Cerutti, in the hotel belonging to
> the Rothschilds, the same house which subsequently

housed the Austrian Consulate, Hortense was eventually delivered of a third boy, whose birth was announced throughout the empire by salvoes of artillery. (1)

However, the future emperor's survival was far from assured. His mother later reported that he was so. . .

> weak that I thought I should lose him directly after his birth. He had to be bathed in wine and to be wrapped in cotton to bring him back to life. I had ceased to think about my own life. Sinister ideas presented to me only the certainty of death. I so thoroughly expected it, that I asked my accoucheur coldly if he could live another day.(1)

He obviously did survive and he proved to be a person endowed with a remarkable memory. Louis could remember farther back than most people claim to be able to. For example, he noted:

> 'The earliest of my recollections goes back to my baptism. Let me say at once that I was baptized at the age of three, in 1810, in the Chapel of the Chateau of

Fontainebleau, The Emperor was my godfather and the Empress Marie Louise my godmother."(2)

The date was November 4, 1810 and the baptism was performed by the eminent Cardinal Fesch. When the young man grew to adulthood he performed all of the deeds expected of an Emperor despite being baptized a Christian.

## THE 19TH CENTURY ANTI-CHRIST

Here are the specifics that made so many people believe that this man was THE true Anti-Christ. First - as to the identifying number 666. Louis Napoleon's name adds up to the infamous 666 in the three major languages in use at the time of the writing of the *Apocalypse.*

His name in Latin would be written as LVDVICV which adds up to 666. His name written in Greek would be Calonmeros which adds up to 666. In Hebrew the letters of his name add up to 666 as well.

It's **VITAL** that the man's name be translated to its Greek, Latin and Hebrew counterpart because these are the three major languages in which the earliest version of the *Apocalypse* was written. In most searches for the Anti-Christ his name is converted to English and this negates the findings.

Resuming the search for 666: there is ONLY ONE PERSON who could meet the following critically important qualification. According to the *Apocalypse* it is imperative that 666 postdate a specific person. Six sixty-six must follow this other person (but yet be the same as him).

The Beast of the Bible must follow a great person who has ruled once and then come back to rule only a short time more. This is a very strict requirement. It is also extremely helpful in that it gives a clue to a particular, specific person in history.

Adding clues together, the next clue is that the Anti-Christ and the person he postdates must have been crowned emperor of the Holy Roman Empire. This is another major clue and when added to the others provides a compelling argument for the Beast's identity.

However, when the final clue is added to all the others it reveals the biblical Anti-Christ's identity beyond a doubt. The Beast must also be a particular person, but at the same time NOT BE this particular person. The words in the *Apocalypse* describe the Beast as a person who is, yet isn't a specific person.

This seeming impossible criteria to meet can actually be met, but met by **ONLY ONE PERSON**.

To reveal this person, his predecessor must be revealed first. Many have claimed that the predecessor IS actually the Beast- the true Anti-Christ. But according to the prophetic specifications he isn't. He is only the predecessor of the beast.

This predecessor person is Napoleon Bonaparte. He was crowned Holy Roman Emperor. He once ruled most of the civilized world, was defeated, then exiled. But he came from exile **TO RULE A SHORT TIME MORE** before his final defeat at Waterloo.

This was the person whom the Anti-Christ was TO FOLLOW. FOLLOW!

This person who follows cannot be just anyone. The Beast must have a specific identity; he has to be a person of dual identity.

The ONLY person who can meet <u>**ALL**</u> of the requirements is Louis Napoleon, later known as *<u>Napoleon III</u>*.

Only Louis Napoleon fits <u>**ALL**</u> of the criteria for the Anti-Christ! Only he could be that unique person who is, and yet isn't. He is Napoleon, yet he isn't Napoleon.

And the facts are that Louis Napoleon was not an unimportant figure at all. He had at his command the most powerful army known to the world at that time. He was emperor of the Holy Roman Empire as well as of France.

Once he assumed full power in 1852 he set Europe aflame with war. In his early days he had acted the part of a benign benefactor, as prophesied in the *Book of Revelation* but then he used the forces at his command to dominate the world.

Important to note is that at the actual historical date when Napoleon III took power in France in 1848 the skies were filled with frightening sights, and many natural disasters were taking place. In 1848 one of the most severe meteor showers ever to occur bombarded both Europe and the United States and a great many people feared that the end of the world had come and hid in shelters.

There were also lunar and solar eclipses as well as earthquakes, volcanoes, and mudslides.

All things taken into consideration, Louis Napoleon fits all the criteria of the Anti-Christ as put forth in prophecy.

He also played part in a form of Armageddon. It will be shown how the fate of the world depended on the outcome of a mighty duel between Abraham Lincoln and Napoleon III.

Also to note are the powerful people assisting Napoleon III in scientific matters who at the least could change one metal into another and also create amazingly powerful weapons unseen in the military before.

Among these people was one of the most mysterious figures in history who is known only as Major Frazer. No one knows who he truly was, where he came from and what eventually became of him. But the powers attributed to him were not of this world. Remember, if this sounds too fantastic, Louis Napoleon was regarded as the Anti-Christ.

This is being highlighted so prominently because millions of people at the time of his rule believed Napoleon III to be the Beast of the Bible and this is a fact of history and should be noted. This book, however, is about fact and will not pursue the prophetic side other than how it affected matters as they unfolded.

## LOUIS'S FAMILY LIFE

Between the years 1808 and 1815 Louis led a type of fairy tale existence. He lived in Paris in the same household as his uncle, Napoleon Bonaparte. Anything he wanted was his. Even adult military men catered to his wishes as if they were toy soldiers.

The future French emperor's memories of this period are striking.

> "I used often to go with my brother, who was three years older than myself, to breakfast with the Emperor. We were introduced into a room looking out on the Tuileries Gardens. Directly the Emperor appeared he would walk straight up to us, take us by the head with both hands and set us standing on the table. This unusual way of lifting us terrified our mother…(2)

But the fairy tale life was drastically to change as his uncle departed on a fateful mission. One of the youthful Louis's most potent memories was of saying goodbye to Napoleon Bonaparte as he was about to depart for the battle of Waterloo in 1815, recorded here by a direct witness.

> 'What's the matter, Louis, and why do you run in here?' the Emperor said. But for some moments Louis could answer only with sobs. Presently, when he had been comforted and reassured a little, he said, '..My governess has just been telling me that you are going to the war. Don't go, don't go.' The child's tears softened the Emperor's manner towards him.
>
> And why don't you want me to go? It's not the first time I've been to the war. Why do you cry? Don't fear;

I shall soon be back.'

'Dear uncle, those wicked Allies will kill you. Let me go with you.'

'The Emperor took the boy upon his knees and pressed him against his heart. Then turning to Soulte:

"Kiss the boy, Marshal. He has a good heart and a noble soul, and will one day, perhaps, be the hope of my race."(1)

That was certainly a prophetic statement by the then Emperor of France about his young nephew whom was only seven years old at the time.

These are clearly not the memories of an ordinary youth. Some may consider these various episodes in his life as demonstrating a positive lifestyle, one of familial closeness and filled with all of the luxuries that a person could desire. Yes, a true fairy tale life. But the problem with fairy tales is that they are not real.

When observed from another angle one might recognize a very perverted lifestyle depicted here. The household in which the future emperor was raised was dysfunctional at best, dominated by megalomaniacs and the worst type of hedonists and pleasure-seekers. They were so overcome by their own self importance that they believed that even a constellation in outer space should be named after them.

> The Napoltonides. When a star of the first magnitude rises in the heavens, we see emerge around it heavenly bodies of less brilliance, so as to form a constellation of which it is the centre. Thus the Napoleonides gravitate about Louis Napoleon. They think the Bourbons have disappeared from the political firmament only to make room for them. They are many in number.(4)

It is difficult to find a conceit that is comparable!

## LINCOLN'S EARLY LIFE

Compare these early days of the future emperor to the boyhood of Abraham Lincoln. Lincoln lived a particularly "normal" life for the times. His father was a rugged outdoorsman who kept his family on the move to find ever better living conditions.

Abraham Lincoln was born on February 12, 1809 to Thomas Lincoln and Nancy Hanks on a 348 acre farm in Nolin Creek which was then in southeast Hardin County, Kentucky. Thomas Lincoln had come with his parents from Virginia and he worked as a farmer and carpenter in the frontier of Kentucky.

The Lincolns named their second son - the first had died in infancy - Abraham out of respect for Lincoln's grandfather who had been killed in an Indian raid in 1786.

Lincoln's first seven years of life were spent in Kentucky on the Sinking Spring Farm that his father had purchased for $200. There was very little glamour in his early life, a time Lincoln described as, "the short and simple annals of the poor."

That was a great understatement. His family was not just poor, it was destitute!

The extent of Lincoln's poverty is seldom highlighted by most writers. He truly grew up in the depths of squalor. Lincoln did not live his early years in a log cabin: that for him would have been a luxury!

Lincoln lived in a three-sided shack. The fourth side was covered with brush, branches and bramble and anything else that would serve as a portable wall. The floor was dirt!

The family did not eat unless they went out and shot their own food. Lincoln's mother could not even afford pins to keep her clothing together. She used thorns instead!

Lincoln's entire family faced the severest types of hardships, struggling day to day for basic survival. These were conquered through perseverance and good old hard work. The deeper hardships of the loss of loved ones, so common amongst the poor in this era, were vanquished by a strengthening of will and character.

In 1818 a disease known as milk sickness struck the area in which the Lincoln's lived. It was a usually fatal condition acquired by drinking the milk of a cow which had eaten white snakeroot, a deadly poison for humans. It was a common illness in the Midwest at that time.

The illness claimed Lincoln's mother, as well as his mother's aunt and uncle in 1818. Twelve-year-old Sarah, Lincoln's older sister by three years, took over the household.

Due to the spread of the milk sickness, Lincoln's father moved the family again, eventually ending up in Illinois. The senior Mr. Lincoln also re-married, returning home from a trip to Kentucky with a woman named Sarah Bush Johnson. Lincoln was devoted to his new mother and was known to refer to her as "my angel mother."

Sarah Bush Lincoln, a widow with a natural son of her own, raised Lincoln as her own. In much later years, she had this to say: "Both were good boys, but I must say - both now being dead that Lincoln was the best boy I ever saw or expected to see."

This is the familial setting of a righteous man, a man of surpassing character. It existed in a world of reality and not fantasy. It endured through the normal sufferings of a backwoods family.

## THE YOUNG ADULT LOUIS NAPOLEON

After Napoleon's defeat at Waterloo, all of the remaining Bonapartes were sent into exile. That included Louis and his mother Hortense. They spent their exile, however, in luxurious accommodations.

His mother, Hortense, spent her time in the salons and attending fancy masquerade balls while her son continued amassing education and acquiring allies. It would seem that he had little to complain about. But complain is mostly what he did.

He saw no other life for himself than that of being the Emperor of France. Despite his claims of hoping to serve the public he was in reality a totally self-involved personality. The future emperor was a narcissist to the highest degree!

For him the years between 1815 and 1830 were years of preparation, preparation to lay siege to the government of France.

At this point it would be instructive to stop and examine the generic personality of a totalitarian ruler. What kind of a person would one expect him to be?

He would certainly be the type of individual who sought total world domination, like the person now being showcased. He would most likely be a person who is very bitter from either imagined or partially genuine past injustices against him. He would be a man at the centre of the worldwide power elite, such as the monarchs of Europe in the 19th century. And he would have an overwhelming - even psychotic - drive to succeed at any costs. The following quote should exemplify this personality type:

> "Dear Mother, to give you a detailed account
> Of my misfortunes is to renew your grief and mine.
> Strong in my conviction, which made me look upon the
> Napoleonic cause as the only national cause of France,
> civilizing cause in Europe, proud of the nobility and
> purity of my intentions, I had quite resolved to raise
> the imperial eagle or fall a victim to my political
> fate."(1)

This sounds like a person with a hugely inflated ego and a serious mother complex. This sounds like a person who will stop at nothing and attempt anything to get what he wants. For further evidence of this, this is one of the most famous quotes made directly by the future emperor:

**The important thing in politics is to reach one's end; the means do not matter.**

He's clearly stating that **THE ENDS JUSTIFY THE MEANS**. And the ends are always and only what is best for HIM.

This brief digression was important at this point to demonstrate how genuinely evil this person was. He is not a poor unfortunate boy who has seen his family thrown into exile and forced from their native land for no valid reason! There IS GOOD REASON!

Many of the quotes that will be attributed to the future emperor will be smothered in self pity and a sense of elitist entitlement. This is important to note because if a listener would accept his words at face value one might view him as a downtrodden figure whose only ultimate goal was for the common good which is how some historians described him. And that's precisely what he wanted his contemporaries to believe. And - for a long period - they did.

**LINCOLN AND LOUIS'S EARLY MILITARY CAREERS**

Both Lincoln and Louis Napoleon had short military careers and the highest rank of each - aside from being respective commanders in chief - was that of captain. Lincoln joined the militia from New Salem, Illinois on April 21, 1832 and was elected by his peers to the position of captain. It would be fair to state that this was his first successful election because rank was gained by election at that time.

According to Lincoln, he later remarked that there had not been "any such success in life which gave me so much satisfaction," as his election to captain.

Ironically, similar words were spoken by the future emperor. He was as thrilled at his rise to captain as had been Lincoln of his election to captain. Louis attained this rank in the Swiss army in 1832, and the event is well documented.

One of his biographers describes the moment:

He has just been gazette a Captain, and cannot
Contain himself for delight.

'I am getting a promotion," he told me with a
smile. 'How high shall I rise, I wonder."

"To an Emperor's epaulettes," I answered.(1)

Although Lincoln did not see any actual fighting in the Black Hawk War, he did help in the burial of soldiers left on the field by Major Isaiah Stillman after the Battle of Stillman's Run.

(Note: in early American nomenclature the work run was used the same as river)

Lincoln returned to New Salem from the Black Hawk War. The common story is that someone stole his horse and that he and a friend named George Harrison canoed and hiked together back home.

Affairs in New Salem went well for Lincoln, now a war veteran. He was only twenty-three-years-old and declared himself a candidate for the Illinois Legislative Assembly as a Whig. One of the platforms he ran on would be the revival of his idea to improve navigation on the Sangamon River to improve trade to the smaller towns.

He lost the overall election against thirteen other opponents which was held on August 6, 1832. But from the New Salem district Lincoln received 277 out of the 300 votes that were cast. But this was Lincoln's first real attempt at politics.

In 1834 Lincoln won election to the Illinois Legislature, again as a Whig and served in successive six terms through 1842.

The Whig Party in America existed from about 1833 until 1856. Its main purpose was to counter Andrew Jackson and the policies of the Democrats. Other than this, the Whigs did not strongly support any particular public policy.

The year 1836 was a very important year for Lincoln because he passed the bar in that year.

It was an extraordinary year for the future Emperor as well. Like Lincoln, Louis Napoleon had by now reached maturity. And Louis had already begun to demonstrate his leanings toward evil.

## THE FIRST COUP

At this stage, both Lincoln and Louis Napoleon are very different people from whom they were shortly to become. Both went under drastic personality changes. Also they were already taking those first steps on that long journey which would eventually lead them to a showdown for world domination.

At this point in his life, Louis Napoleon was a buffoon with delusions of grandeur. And Lincoln was a struggling politician with a brilliant legal mind but little success yet. What is it that will cause such amazing changes in both men?

Napoleon's first attempt to take over the government of France gave him his first lesson in tactics. It was an ill-conceived plot that would have been comical if it hadn't been so pathetic. Actually, it was comical.

The would-be coup will be laid out in detail, to which I will add critical commentary. Remember, Louis Napoleon is the same man who will later conquer almost half the world! How did this buffoon become a great leader if not through the outside help of an unusual nature?

Most history books report the story of Louis's first coup attempt in a straightforward way. On October 30 in 1836 at 6 in the morning Louis Napoleon appeared outside a National Guard garrison in Strasbourg, France.

He was attired in full Napoleonic attire and demanded to be recognized as the new emperor of the country. It was characterized as a ludicrous affair and is probably where he was first given the nickname of rampole, which means a mad fool. The result was his arrest and imprisonment.

At this time in the life of Abraham Lincoln he was working as a surveyor. On the same day that Louis Napoleon was attempting his first coup, Abraham Lincoln had stopped over night at the Deer Lick Tavern in Oakford, Illinois on route to survey the town of Bath. Quite a difference in lifestyle.

There are differing versions of the attempted coup by Louis. His version is very different from the others. He wrote a detailed description of what he thought was actually taking place.

What is to follow is Louis's version of what happened that day beginning at six in the morning, along with clarifying comments by this book's author.

The description of the assault on the barracks is a rather lengthy portion from his memoirs, but it is exceptionally vital and extremely interesting both from the point of view of looking into the workings of a deranged and evil mind and from the point of view of a curious adventure in history. Also, if viewed for what it TRULY was, it was quite a humorous event.

Louis Napoleon:

At last six o'clock struck! Never did the striking of a clock rouse so violent a commotion within me; but a moment more, and the reveille from the Austerlitz Barracks set my heart beating more wildly still. The great moment was at hand. Next instant no small commotion reached our ears from the street: soldiers tramped by shouting, horsemen dashed full gallop past our windows. I sent an officer to find out the reason: was it the Headquarter Staff that was already aware of our plans. Had we been discovered? He came back directly to tell me the noise came from a number of troopers the Colonel was sending to fetch their horses, which were stabled outside the barracks. (1)

(Author's note: this wild commotion in the street had nothing to do with Louis Napoleon's scheme, yet he made it seem so. It is a product of his delusional thinking. Basically, he was marching down the street in the midst of a common crowd with only a couple of accomplices beside him.)

"The intervening space was short, and was soon crossed. The regiment was drawn up in parade order in

the barrack-square (of the Austerlitz Barracks) inside the
gates; on the grass were stationed forty mounted
artillerymen. (1)

(Author's note: at this point Louis Napoleon walks into the garrison and announces that he has come to take over the government. None of the soldiers knew who this man was or why he was there.)

"Soldiers of the 4th regiment of artillery! A great
revolution is accomplishing at this moment. You see
before you the nephew of the Emperor Napoleon I.,
come to champion the rights of the people; the
people and the army can count on me.
Soldiers! you will feel, as your commander does, all the
grandeur of the enterprise you are about to undertake,
all the sacredness of the cause you are about to defend.
Soldiers! Can the nephew of the Emperor Napoleon
count on you.'(1)

(Author's note: he received a disbelieving silence which was tantamount to roaring laughter at this foolish display)

"Arrived in the courtyard of the General's house,
I climb the stairs, followed by MM. Vaudrey, Parquin
and two officers. The General was not yet dressed. I
say to him: 'General, I come to you as a friend; I
should be grieved to raise our old flag, the tricolor,
without a gallant soldier like yourself; the garrison is
on my side, make up your mind to follow me.' He was
shown the eagle, but he pushed it away and said:

> 'Prince, they have deceived you; the army knows its duty, and I shall very soon convince you it is so.' Thereupon I withdrew, issuing orders to leave an artillery picket to keep guard over him. (1)

(Author's note: He was basically told to get lost! He did get lost, but not before leaving an imaginary guard over the commandant. The fact is: no one had joined his coup!)

> "We resumed our march. We turned out of the main street and made our way into the Finkmatt Barracks by the narrow lane leading to it from the Faubourg de Pierre. It is a large building constructed in a sort of blind alley; the space in front is too confined to allow a regiment to be drawn up in review order. Seeing myself thus shut in between the ramparts and the barrack buildings, I perceived that the plan agreed upon had not been followed. (1)

(Author's note: there had not been a plan. How could there have been? No one knew why he was there.)

> So confined was the space that each of us was lost in the press. The populace that had mounted on the wall, began to throw stones at the infantry, the gunners indeed to use their pieces; but we stopped that, for we saw in a moment we should have killed numbers of people. I saw the Colonel first arrested by the infantry, then released by the artillerymen. For myself, I was being borne down by a crowd of men who, recognizing me, leveled their bayonets at me; I parried their thrusts with my sword, trying to appease them the while, till

the gunners came up and dragged me under shelter
of their muskets and set me in their midst. Then I
rushed forward, with three or four non-commissioned
officers, towards the mounted artillerymen to get hold
of a horse, all the infantry-men at my heels.

I found myself jammed in between the horses and wall
So that I could not stir. Then up came the fellows from
...sides, seized hold of me, and led me off to the guard-
room. On entering, I found M. Parquin there; I held
out my hand to him. Accosting me with an air of calm
and quiet resignation, he said: 'Prince, we shall be shot,
but we shall die in a good cause. 'Yes' I answered
him,' we have failed in a noble and a glorious enter-
prize.'

"At the gaol, during the formalities of our admission,
we all met again. M. de Querelles, seizing my hand and
pressing it, said out loud: 'Prince, in spite of our defeat,
still proud of what I have done.' I was subjected
to an examination; I was calm and resigned; my mind
was made up. I was asked the following questions:
What induced you to act as you have done.' 'My
political opinions,' I replied, 'and my desire once again
to see my country, of which the invasion of foreigners
had robbed me.' (1)

How serious of an assault on the walls of the garrison really was this? The impartial accounts which called it a ludicrous stunt are a more apt description than Louis's wild concoction!

According to even Louis's own accounts, it seems clear that the only other person who was **REALLY** taking part in the coup *with him* was his old friend Vaudrey. It was later learned from a former lover of Vaudrey's that he had informed the government about the plot and that the garrison had been prepared for the so-called coup.

Thus it is clear that the supposed support that had been gathered for Louis during his early morning march to the garrison was a fabrication of his own mind and that the only people assisting him were in fact traitors to "his" cause.

What was the purpose of the coup? Louis Philippe had recently crowned himself king of France. Louis Napoleon was hoping to install himself as emperor - despite his claims at the ensuing trial. How was this going to benefit the common man and bring him more liberty?

Louis Napoleon was quickly brought to trial. His ultimate judge was the king of France who dealt with him with extreme leniency. His offence was punishable by execution but the penalty Louis received was to be exiled again. This time – he was sent to the United States and he stood on American soil at the same time as Abraham Lincoln. But they never "formally" met.

Considering how absurd his first coup attempt had been, a person must believe that in order to proceed with his plans for world dominion as he did he had somehow gained some form of powerful support.

After the trial, Louis Napoleon was taken under arrest to the citadel Port-Louis near Lorient where he awaited exile. The first landing in North America was at Norfolk, Virginia on March 30, 1837.

## THE EMPEROR IN AMERICA

Are there powers unknown to us that set in motion events that all lead to a planned outcome? What took place during Louis Napoleon's one and only trip to the United States seems to imply there is.

Some people call this force for designing the future, God. Some call it Divine Intelligence. Some atomic-consciousness. No matter what it is called it certainly seemed to be in play in regards to the lives of Lincoln and Napoleon III and how they were to be associated.

While it is true that the two men never physically met each other they did have acquaintances in common on the American side of the Atlantic. Some of them will take part in highly significant state matters in the future, and some of them will simply be clues in demonstrating how the lives of these two men were destined to intertwine in the most extraordinary ways.

During Napoleon III's visit to the United States he proved himself to be an utterly unprincipled, uncouth lowlife! If this sounds like biased reporting it isn't intended to be. It is meant to provide an equalising factor to the massive propaganda that Napoleon III had released to the world, claiming that he was an upstanding and decent human being whose sole concern was the welfare of his subjects.

When Louis came to America he met with a number of senators and statesman, one of the most important of whom was a man named Watson Webb. Webb would one day be a highly placed diplomat in Lincoln's future administration who would once again come into contact with the devious Frenchman under critical conditions. These conditions centred on France's occupation of Mexico in 1862 and the possibility of intervention by the European power in the War Between the States with dire effects for the Union.

As typical for Louis, he stayed amongst the highest of society, associating with the wealthiest and loftiest placed people in the land.

Among the people he socialised with were: Washington Irving, the Williamses of Cincinnati, Generals Wilson, Winfield Scott and Webb, in addition to Chancellor Kent, O. Seymour, and the Livingston and Hamilton families. Many of these names mean little to people in the 21st century but they were all very prominent in the mid 1800's.

Washington Irving and the Alexander Hamilton Family are immediately recognized by most Americans. So too would be General Winfield Scott, who would become famous for his roles in the Mexican-American War as well as the War Between the States. Thus, he too would be another connection between Lincoln and the Emperor.

What follows is a brief synopsis of Louis Napoleon's visit to America, memorialised not many years after the event:

> In New York Louis stopped at Washington Hall, a hotel built in 1810, which occupied about half the block on the east side of Broadway between Chambers and Reade Streets. The building was then one of the finest in the city. There were no better club houses in New York at that early day, and the celebrated "Bread and Cheese Club" founded by James Fenimore Cooper in 1824 met there. **One of the houses on the same block contained two stores about twelve feet wide, one of which was occupied by A. T. Stewart.** In 1844, Stewart bought Washington Hall, and on the site, which was finally extended so as to include the entire block front, he erected a fine marble building for his store. When he moved up to Tenth Street in 1862, the store was turned into an office building. It is now owned by Frank A. Munsey and occupied by "The Sun and New York Herald." (2)

The part about his visit with A. T. Stewart is the most astounding of all! It represents a connection between Lincoln and the Emperor which almost leaves one with mouth agape. Why?

In 1876 and 1877 both Abraham Lincoln and A.T. Stewart's corpses were the objects of kidnapping attempts within months of the other. What are the odds against such a random similarity of future events? In some inexplicable way the simple fact that the Emperor stayed at the home of A.T. Stewart while in this country creates another eerie thread to Abraham Lincoln.

Turning to - for lack of a better word - romance, Louis Napoleon was very active in this endeavor when he visited America, regardless of the fact that he had a wife.

When he wasn't socialising with the well-placed people in New York, Louis Napoleon was carousing at a sleazy bar on Grand Street in Manhattan. Being the man that he was, Louis had begun an affair with a prostitute named Josephine Ballabo. The affair had to be broken off abruptly because Louis Napoleon was forced to return home after only a few weeks in the United States due to the sudden ill health of his mother, Hortense.

The future Emperor's affair with his prostitute friend spotlights the theme of this book **PRECISELY**. It shows the two men in juxtaposition: the decent, God-fearing Abraham Lincoln as against the immoral, deceitful Louis Napoleon.

It seems that for one to exist, so must the other. Evil must have its counterpart. This is not a scientific observation. It is not even provable. But that does not prevent this concept from being true! Recall Thessalonians.

While Honest Lincoln was attempting to foster an innocent, loving relationship with an upstanding young woman, the sex-crazed, godless soon-to-be ruler of France was having an affair with a woman of the streets.

Of course, having an affair with one particular woman does not necessarily make a person sex-crazed. However, Louis Napoleon will prove to be a womanizer who regularly cheated on his wife Eugenia and who employed one of his officials to acquire females for his pleasure - to pimp for him!

Louis Napoleon's opinions about women aren't surprising, considering how he abused those of this gender. One of his most self-elevating quotes in this regard ran thus: "It is usually the man who attacks. As for me, I defend myself, and I often capitulate." This seemingly was supposed to be witty.

Apparently, then, Louis Napoleon's wife was one of the few women to whom he need not worry about capitulating. According to her, the thought of having sex with him was, "disgusting."

## THE ROMANTIC LINCOLN?

The purpose is to draw comparisons and provide parallels between Lincoln and Napoleon III. In the area of romance probably the only things that Lincoln and Louis Napoleon had in common were bad marriages. In each case, insanity was a problem: Lincoln had his Mary, and Eugenia had her Louis.

The quotes and letters from Lincoln that follow should suffice to document his difficult romantic life.

"Although I seem to others to enjoy life rapturously at times, yet when I am alone I am so depressed that I am afraid to trust myself to carry a pocket-knife." (5)

This was said by Lincoln after the passing of Ann Rutledge, the woman that some people claimed he never knew!

As good as a quote is a letter that Lincoln wrote to a young woman he was attempting to "woo."

> What I do wish is, that our further acquaintance shall depend upon yourself. If such further acquaintance would contribute nothing to your happiness, I am sure it would not to mine. If you feel yourself in any degree bound to me, I am now willing to release you, provided you wish it; while,

on the other hand, I am willing, and even anxious to bind you faster, if I can be convinced that it will, in any considerable degree, add to your happiness. This, indeed, is the whole question with me. Nothing would make me more miserable than to believe you miserable---nothing more happy, than to know you were so.

Lincoln: "I have now come to the conclusion never again to think about marrying, and for this reason; I can never be satisfied with anyone who would be blockhead enough to have me."

On Friday, November 4, 1842, Lincoln reluctantly and with an aching heart, asked Mary Todd to be his wife. While Lincoln was putting on his best clothes on the evening of his wedding, and blacking his boots, a little boy rushed in and asked him where he was going. Lincoln replied: "To hell, I suppose." Lincoln's best man testified that he "looked and acted as if he were going to the slaughter."(5)

On the day of the scheduled marriage, Lincoln did not show up. They found him hours later sitting in his office, talking incoherently. His friends feared he was losing his mind. Mary Todd's relatives declared that he was already insane and should be put away. (5)

Why did Lincoln marry Mary Todd if she made him so utterly miserable? The answer seems to be fate. It had been implied that he would never have been president if he had not married this particular woman. That is because Mary Todd relentlessly drove Abraham Lincoln into seeking the presidency. And if he had not won the presidency there would not have been the confrontation with the Emperor that would change the world. Fate? The will of God? Atomic consciousness? Is there a difference?

## NOT ANOTHER COUP?

Louis Napoleon returned to Europe to be at his mother's side at her deathbed. Afterwards he remained in Europe and travelled extensively through the various lands, attempting to amass allies.

Becoming bored with this, Louis decided that it was once again time to try to wrest control of the French government from its current leaders.

Apparently, his mind was not capable yet of thinking along the lines of legally reaching his goals by doing something like running for election. Admittedly, that might have been a little difficult for someone who was exiled from his home country.

But once again the point here is to note how totally inept Louis Napoleon was at this time in his life - and he is an adult! How could such a fool suddenly become a brilliant tactician who takes over France then conquers most of the Western world? How!

This coup attempt was even more ludicrous and less destined for success than his previous attempt. What follows is a description of how the coup was prepared, based on direct observation by one of the parties to it. It is also a very amusing tale.

### AUGUST 6, 1840

(Louis Napoleon has) purchased guns in Birmingham and uniforms at the March du Temple in Paris. Servants have been engaged in France and conveyed to London, where he has also had the uniforms forwarded. Dr. Conneau has sewn on the buttons. He has procured a printing-press, and is printing off his proclamations himself.

> Louis Napoleon has chartered, under an assumed name, a steamer, the Edinburgh Castle. He has contrived to complete all preparations without the Cabinets of London and Paris knowing one word of his projects. Normanby, Guizot, have not seen a thing. It is like a fairy tale !

> We are going aboard immediately. To-morrow we
> shall be off Boulogne. Who knows if, the day after,
> Louis Napoleon will not be on the throne of France? (2)

This was all the planning they thought that they needed to set up a new king on the throne of France! This sounds either like a bunch of children at play or a group of psychotic adults with delusions of grandeur and an awful lot of money.

What this was in reality was a bunch of paid servants attired in military-like uniforms who accompanied Louis through the streets in the guise of a local uprising. That's the reality of the situation. There was not a true military man among them, accepting for Louis himself and his nearest comrades.

The plan was to disembark with this party of sixty-two fake revolutionaries at the port of Boulogne, France, march through town drawing huge crowds of support, and take over the army garrison. What happened was: none of the citizens of the town paid any attention to Louis Napoleon and his mercenary mob, the gates of the garrison were closed and remained closed, and Louis marched with his group to the top of a nearby hill. This was where the imperial flag flew and Louis thought that he would be successful if he took control of the hilltop!

At this point, the guards from the garrison were loosened upon them and this motley group of servants dressed as soldiers were gunned down and forced into the river, where they were used as target practice. The fledging emperor was dragged from the scene kicking and screaming by his close friends. This is literally what happened!

The following is a description by one who was part of the rabble.

> I make a last attempt to raise the citizens, and so find myself separated from my friends, who reach the shore, pursued by the soldiers and the National Guard, which is sent to arrest them. The Prince and some of my friends, it appears, threw themselves into the sea to escape; but they were cowardly enough to pepper them from the cliffs, like water-fowl. Voisin was hit twice; Hun was drowned; another was killed; others fell seriously wounded, and lay fainting and covered with blood. Persigny, Conneau, Mesonan, captured by gendarmes in boats, were brought back to the beach, and all my comrades were made prisoners. For the good of the cause I thought it best to escape, mixing with my contingent of "shouters," and distributing money among them to win their connivance. So here I am, the same as after Strasbourg, alone, abandoned, frustrated....(1)

Napoleon III's followers were forced into the river where the French guards used them as target practice! How to save face in such a situation? Maybe a timely slogan would help, Louis's people thought. So they tried:

> Success to the brave, the proverb says . . . and
> also the cup of gall, sometimes! (1)

On this same date in history Abraham Lincoln signed off with other law partners on a $10,000 bail bond for one of their clients.

The inconsistencies of Louis Napoleon have been noted, now it's time to take a look at Lincoln. There aren't any signs that he would ever become a successful politician. Actually, at this point Lincoln is completely devoted to his law practice.

He too will go though a drastic change which will one day bring him into confrontation with the Emperor. Will this also be a matter of divine intervention?

## LOUIS ESCAPES

Punishment for his second attempted coup for Louis Napoleon was supposedly incarceration for life in the ancient fortress of Ham. In reality this location was a vast villa where many heads of state had stayed. It was a luxurious prison.

Louis Napoleon enjoyed a six-year-long vacation here. He wrote several publications, saw many friends - most of them of the privileged classes - and even took the time to father two boys by the combination laundress/cleaning woman who worked at the facilities. Her name was Alexandrine Vergeot. Yes - Napoleon III capitulated to the advances of a lowly laundress, showing himself to be completely egalitarian where sexual matters are concerned.

Louis of course was a full grown adult at this period in his life. Perhaps a physical description would be in order at this point. He was of average height but had an unusual build in that Louis had a long torso and short legs. His eyes were gray and he had a large nose. His bushy moustache was of an auburn hue. By all accounts, Louis Napoleon was quite underwhelming. But it didn't detract from his sex drive nor did it seem to make him less appealing to the womenfolk.

It was probably with a great sense of condescension that Louis "capitulated" to the cleaning woman/laundress whom he nonetheless found to be:

> To his taste, and she made no resistance, but returned him love for love. It is a case of genuine mutual affection. She is not pretty, but her blue eyes and fresh complexion are fascinating. This time the idyll is crossed by no disappointment. Two children, both boys, Eugene and Louis, are the result of the daily visits of the sabot-maker's daughter to Louis Napoleon's chamber. (2)

What eventually became of these playthings of Louis's?

... **Alexandrine Vergeot** married Napoleon III' s foster-brother. She died in poverty in Paris in 1886.(3)

Alexandrine died in poverty. Apparently, Louis forgot all about this great love of his life. But the cleaning woman was not the only woman at Ham to receive his special attention, there were others as well.

Louis Napoleon was acquiring various nicknames now. The first one - Mad Fool - came from his first coup attempt. The next one he earned while at Ham was: Baron of the Ramparts. This came about due to his many frequent appearances riding and waving to the ladies on the ramparts of the massive estate.

Actually, it was at Ham that he got most of his nicknames. The next one was "Bandinguet" because of the way in which he finally escaped.

It was a simple matter of disguising himself as a stone mason named Bandinguet - a real stone mason doing repairs on Louis's apartment - and slipping out of the fortress while the guards were on a coffee break. A couple of friends were waiting for him on the grounds outside to drive him away.

Many history books declare his escape from Ham as "daring." And it even won Louis another nickname, "Man of Destiny."

Yet, he was still a sex maniac and a buffoon. How indeed would this person attain the exalted position of emperor? This is even as much of a mystery as the sheer fact of it.

## 1846 - 1848

These are two years of extreme importance for both Abraham Lincoln and Louis Napoleon. This is when signs of their turning points began to appear.

Is it just coincidence that these two years were particularly critical to both men? Or was it that they were both being prepared for the cosmic battle that was to come and would both be ready at the right time?

In 1846 Lincoln had been elected to the United States House of Representatives as a Whig. He would serve for only these two years which did not make for a lasting political career. The country was in the midst of war with Mexico and Lincoln held the unpopular view of being against the conflict and that was his only great issue while in office.

Lincoln was particularly angry at President James Polk and his policies. He was spiteful and vindictive and spoke out with open hostility as a typical politician might and not as the even tempered Lincoln most people have come to know. In reality, Lincoln was rather a hothead at this time in his life.

In regards to the Mexican-American War Lincoln contended that the United States was the aggressor and to prove this point he diligently sought out the exact **SPOT** on which the war began. Lincoln claimed that this spot was actually on Mexican land and that we had invaded it, making the United States the aggressor. This by the way won him a particular nickname among floor Democrats: "Spotty Lincoln."

It was Lincoln's contention that President Polk far overstepped his powers by going to war with Mexico, and he took the president to task. A young and angry Abraham Lincoln marched onto the floor of the U.S. House of Representatives and verbally attacked President James Polk:

> As I have before said, he knows not where he is. He is a bewildered, confounded, and miserably perplexed man. God grant he may be able to show, there is not something about his conscious, more painful than all his mental perplexity! God of heaven has forgotten to defend the weak and the innocent, and permitted the strong band of murderers and demons from hell to kill men, women, and children and lay waste and pillage the land of the just."

The land to which he was referring was Mexico. The murderers and demons were President Polk and his top generals who were also guilty of war crimes, he believed. This is as strong a statement as Abraham Lincoln has ever made.

Lincoln joined with 81 other Whigs and 81 Democrats to create an amendment which was passed but was never voted upon, declaring that the war was "a war unnecessarily and unconstitutionally begun by the president of the United States."

It has been said that no one in Washington was really paying any heed to the young congressman from Illinois. However, the people back in Illinois were paying close attention to him. Most of them were outraged by his stance against the war.

Some of the remarks made against Lincoln were brutal. One person denounced his attacks on the war effort as the "treasonable assaults of guerrillas at home." Another referred to him as a "slanderer of the president." A still stronger epitaph against him was to be called one of the "defenders of butchery at the Alamo." And, finally, a displeased Illinoisan said that Lincoln was a "traducer of the heroism at San Jacinto." San Jacinto was an early Texican victory over the Mexican army in 1836.

The damage being done to Lincoln's reputation was so severe that his law partner Mr. Herndon suggested that he cease and desist his opposition to the war. If he did not, it may amount to political suicide.

Lincoln took his friend's advice and remained silent on the war from that point onward.

But Lincoln's protests against the war had genuine prophetic value. He warned against the havoc that this war would have on Mexico's economic and political system. A crushing defeat would leave Mexico vulnerable to attack by an outside force which would then become a natural threat to the United States.

In 1862 this outside force would in fact occupy Mexico. And it would be under the direction of the Emperor of France!

Maybe that was the reason for Lincoln's uncharacteristic political venom against the Mexican-American war. Could it be that he subconsciously saw what would happen in the future and felt extreme frustration about not being able to do anything about it? Could it have been divine inspiration that allowed Lincoln to see the potential danger?

The United States defeated Mexico in the war. The result left Mexico in a greatly vulnerable condition as predicted by Lincoln. It was this which eventually allowed France to take over Mexico and place Maximilian in control of that country, leaving a hostile European nation on our Southern border during the time of our Civil War. Is this the future that Lincoln was somehow able to see?

While it is true that Lincoln seemed endowed with a special vision, it was also true at this point in life he was not a very good politician. He certainly was no one's choice to become president of the United States. Certainly no one could have expected him to also be the founder of a new political party - The Republican Party.

Something happened to change Lincoln into a political genius and Louis Napoleon into a ruthless world conqueror. Oddly, it may have been the exact same event that changed both of them!

## TRANSFORMATION

Louis Napoleon fled to England from HAM in 1848. For the first several months he suffered from a mysterious ailment. He spent this time reading, doing some type of scientific experiments, and refraining from scheming and plotting.

When his health improved, he resumed his old style of life as described by one of his biographers:

> The first appearance of Louis Napoleon in London after his escape was very dramatic. It was the night of the 26 May 1846, and a large party was being given at Gore House, the residence of Lady Blessington, when he suddenly made his appearance. No one had heard of his arrival in the city. He was again well received by his old friends, and he made up for his five years of seclusion by a furious pursuit of pleasure.

46

> In the evening he went to the theatre or opera,
> or dropped in at one of his clubs for a quiet game of
> whist, which he had learned to play at Ham. In brief,
> he led the life of a man-about-town. (2)

Yes, still the flighty man-about-town. Still the child, still the buffoon. Still chasing women like a dog in rut:

> At this same time there was much talk of a marriage
> between the Prince and a young and charming
> English girl, Miss Emmy Bowles. By a very curious
> coincidence she was then living with her brother-in-
> law at Camden Place, Chislehurst...
> The project was given up when Miss Bowles heard
> of the liaison between the Prince and Miss Howard. (4)

At first this seems like just a simple, innocent report of a soap-opera-like event. But in reality it is a link to a remarkable prediction for the future.

A gentleman who resided in the Camden Place neighborhood purchased this Chislehurst home with a particular intent in mind. The man had had a premonition that at the conclusion of Napoleon III's reign Louis would return here to die. That was twenty-four years before the fact, and makes the Chislehurst connection much more than a mere coincidence because this is where Napoleon III did pass away.

47

Another coincidence? Or another prophecy that was fulfilled?

The change that transformed Louis Napoleon from buffoon to tactical mastermind took place instantly, literally over night, on February 24, 1848. It can be pinpointed that precisely.

What happened? The then reigning monarch of France, Louis Philippe, abdicated. He simply abandoned the throne in the midst of the people's revolution which was raging through Paris. And at that moment, his leadership and ruling powers were transferred to Louis Napoleon, soon to name himself Napoleon III.

Even this had been predicted!

> The peace of Europe and the world apparently rests upon the life of a single wise old man, Louis Philippe. When the obstacle presented by this modern day Sobrino shall have been removed, the demons of discord, now scarcely repressed, will be let loose. Revolution will elevate the revived Bonaparte of the day, to the imperial throne of military despotism. (6)

This was foretold in a book written before the event by Sarah P. Walsworth, titled "Destined Monarch of the World." She even declared that it would occur during a revolution.

What follows is a short description of the abdication of King Louis Philippe on February 24, 1848.

It is currently reported that the King wished to mount his horse and ride to the barricades, surrounded by his sons and some of his Generals. Thiers persuaded him not to. "All is over, Sire," was his word. The little man can see nothing but troubled waters, and is preparing to cast his line in them. At the Tuileries Louis Philippe is surrounded by none but pusillanimous, ineffectual cowards.

Girardin appears again and repeats his old song: "Abdicate, abdicate, Sire!" The rattle of musketry outside announces that the fatal hour has struck. Crimieux presents a sheet of paper. Montpensier slips it in front of his father and offers him a pen. The King looks in his face, then weakly: "You wish me to?"

He traces a few lines rapidly with a feverish hand. He signs, and eagerly Crimieux seizes the act ofabdication, carries it away with him, and starts off to show it to the people.

Louis Philippe is no longer King of France. He has left Paris. On quitting the Tuileries, he found carriages waiting at the base of the obelisque in the Place de la Concorde and stowed himself and his family in them a dynasty removing without tuck of drum or blare of trumpet! The people has taken possession of the Palace, which is sacked and pillaged; thieves caught in the act are shot. Comedy succeeds tragedy. The mob takes turns to sit on the red velvet seat of the throne. They strike up the "Marseillaise," and an Italian plays the accompaniment on Marie Amlie's piano. (1)

This was an account of the scene of the revolution of 1848 by Baron D'Ambes. It took place as suddenly as that!

When Louis Napoleon changed, so did Abraham Lincoln. Why? Some religiously inclined might say in order to provide for the concept spoken of in Thessalonians and other Old Testament texts. When a man of goodness arises, he will be countered by a man of equal evil, or vice versa. The idea is the same.

> The manifestation of Antichrist or the Man of Sin, as foretold in 2 Thessalonians. "That day (the day of Christ) shall not come, except there come THE EMPEROR - and that Man of Sin be revealed, the son of perdition, who opposeth and exceedeth himself above all that is called God, or that is worshipped..."(6)

In this case, Lincoln (non-divine, of course) is the stand-in for Jesus and Louis Napoleon represents the Emperor in duality of prophecy fashion.

The suddenly changed behavior of both Louis Napoleon and Abraham Lincoln at the same time has to be acknowledged as quite startling whatever the cause!

Louis Napoleon becomes a brilliant tactician and military strategist. What about Lincoln?

Lincoln's view of those who had been in charge of the Mexican-American war totally changed. Totally!

No longer did he disparage President Polk or his top generals. Just the opposite. Lincoln began a fierce political campaign in favor of one of the top military leaders of the war - Zachary Taylor.

This is a fact! Lincoln went on the stump to feverishly promote Taylor for president. Note this portion of one of Lincoln's speeches which was meant to elevate Taylor while making light of his opponent, Cass:

> "By the way, Mr. Speaker, did you know I am a military hero? Yes, sir, in the days of the Black Hawk war, I fought, bled, and came away. Speaking of General Cass's career, reminds me of my own. I was not at Stillman's defeat, but I was about as near it as Cass was to Hull's surrender; and, like him, I saw the place very soon afterward......
>
> If General Cass went in advance of me picking whortleberries, I guess I surpassed him in charges upon the wild onions. If he saw any live fighting Indians, it was more than I did, but I had a good many bloody struggles with the mosquitoes; and, although I never fainted from loss of blood, I can truly say I was often very hungry.
>
> If ever I should conclude to doff whatever our Democratic friends may suppose there is of black-cockade Federalism about me, and, thereupon

> they shall take me up as their candidate for the Presidency, I protest that they shall not make fun of me as they have of General Cass by attempting to write me into a military hero."

Yes, this actually was a speech in favor of Taylor, and it was quite well received. Remember, this was the man who a few months earlier Lincoln had referred to as leading a band of:

> "Murderers and demons from hell to kill men, women, and children and lay waste and pillage the land of the just."

Quite a change of attitude! Suddenly, Lincoln begins to act like an even-tempered politician. But he makes the choice to use decency and humanity to guide his work rather than, as many politicians, adopting a method of scheming and conniving to get as much for himself as he could.

Lincoln will later enter the presidency with the highest standards and ideals that any one at the time could have imagined!

Two of the main characters of this work have been accounted for. What of Pope Pius IX and the mysterious Major Frazer?

## REST OF THE EQUATION

When Pius IX was installed he entered his office with highly popular liberal ideals. He was a champion of the common person, willing to help even the smallest of God's children. The people adored him.

But at roughly the same time that Louis Napoleon and Lincoln underwent their transformations so did he. A complete and total change of personality. What are the odds that this type of change should occur to these three men at this specific time (1848-1850) in history!

Overnight, Pope Pius IX had changed from a defender of human rights to a man who wanted to see the abolishment of all liberties. This is not speculation or a mere assumption. It happened after he had returned to Rome from an exile forced upon him by the Austrians when they overtook the Holy city.

Pius no longer was feared by all the monarchs of Europe because he no longer championed the common man but supported the privileged classes. Pope Pius now believed that the common man should not have any rights except those given him by his masters. The Pope's rule of the Church became rigid and devoid of any compassion.

The Emperor Louis Napoleon and Pope Pius IX have been described in almost identical terms by various people, which seems peculiar. Did they share a common psychopathic personality trait? What follows are independently provided descriptions of each man.

Pope Pius IX:

When bishops displeased him, he ordered them
to kiss his feet. He warned Jews who annoyed
him to "Take care, or I could make you go back
into your hole." It was common for him to go into
rages, yet be alternately kind and cruel to
subordinates.

Napoleon III:

When I think about it, I find the Emperor
enigmatic and singular and yet, I know him! It is not
easy to read such a nature, for it is not often in the
depths what it appears on the surface.
He has unexpected moods of coldness and of kindness,
a habit of fixing on you a scrutinizing and embarrassing
gaze even when you might think that (after so many
years) you had his entire confidence. One moment
He is masterful and harsh, the next astonishingly

kind.(4)

Along with what had just been noted, the pope had become blatantly anti-Semitic, being well-known for a despicable affair in which he forced a Jewish orphan to renounce his natural religion before the world and accept Catholicism in its stead.

This pope was also anti-Masonic, a stance which certainly would find displeasure with the architect of the universe. His raving against the Masons was part of a long list of divisive arguments that he proclaimed in an official document. It was called his Syllabus of Errors and the lengthy document was little more than a manifesto of hate against various groups and beliefs.

This is also the pope who decided that all popes are infallible. It is he who produced the Papal Bull to that effect. Pope Pius IX also gave the Catholic Church the concept of the Immaculate Conception.

These are two of the most important doctrines of the Roman Catholic Church. And even though they were handed down by the pope, they were not readily accepted by Catholics. In fact, many people in the Roman Church opposed them.

Many Catholics balked at the idea that any human being could be termed infallible for any reason. The concept of the Immaculate

Conception did not meet with wide acceptance either. Part of the reason for this was the off-hand way in which the pope announced a major change in a belief system, causing many to tremble with uncertainty about the very sanity of the pontiff.

Having Pope Pius IX on the throne had enormous consequences for Abraham Lincoln, too. Pope Pius IX was in favor of slavery. Yes! This pope praised the institution of slavery. It was his position that the slaves had a better standard of living as slaves than they had in their native land where they pranced around like semi-human creatures, according to him.

Slavery was actually the best thing that could happen to them. They would be forced to learn the teachings of the Church and give up their old heathen ways.

Pope Pius IX was strongly opposed to Abraham Lincoln. The pope openly favored the South when the War Between the States broke out, claiming that the Union was trying to crush an independent state.

In its broadest definition, slavery was the centre of the battle between Lincoln, the Emperor and Pope Pius IX.

Could the pope be trusted? Was he mad? Obsessed? In league with the Devil? Many thought he was all of these things.

## MAJOR FRAZER

This is one of the most mysterious men in history. Practically nothing is known about him which is why little specifically will be reported about him.

What is known are the results of relationships that people have had from contact with this man. He became a vital but wholly illusive figure in Napoleon III's government and is mentioned but once.

However, the things that have been attributed to him are astounding. These will be dealt with at the proper time. This is meant only as a brief introduction to the man with much more to follow.

## THE NEW LOUIS NAPOLEON

Louis Napoleon's amazing metamorphosis occurred when he spiritually assumed his powers from the dethroned King Louis Philippe. This has already been corroborated in a number of ways.

Louis did not put this new ability into play immediately but - unlike his former self - he waited for the proper time. This in itself showed the immense change that had come over him, the leader of two previous foolish coup attempts at a whim!

Louis Philippe abdicated with the outbreak of the Revolution of 1848. At this point, a provisional government was installed. It was in October of 1848 that Louis Napoleon attempted his initial legal entrance into the French government by standing for election as a lowly Department head (something like a US Representative).

Fate broke in at this point to save him. By law, neither he nor any other Bonaparte even had a right to be in the country.

The first important test Louis Napoleon was to face came on October 9th. A vote was going to be held with the purpose of declaring members of the former imperial and royal families of France ineligible as candidates for the presidency of the Republic. If this vote had passed, the hopes of a Napoleon III would be vanquished.

Louis Napoleon was not even going to be allowed to speak due to certain floor rules that had been agreed to, however, a supporter of his who was allowed to speak yielded his time to Louis. Whether or not this idea was original to Louis's political backer or was placed there by another source can never be known.

58

Louis Napoleon then proceeded to give a rambling, disjointed speech which did not make very much sense. Not only that, he gave it with a hint of a German accent, a speaking trait he had developed due to residing so long in Germanic speaking countries.

Louis Napoleon seemed like such a pathetic figure that the man who had introduced the amendment to bar him from ever obtaining the office of president withdrew the amendment because it seemed so absurd that such a man could ever become president. What harm could this confused Louis Napoleon be?

Of course, the confused speech of Louis Napoleon's was planned. He presented exactly the non-threatening figure that he intended to present. The way was opened for him to become president.

Was this more coincidence? Did there just happen by chance to be a supporter of the Emperor's on the floor at the auspicious time or, as suggested earlier, was the idea of yielding the floor placed there by another source?

Oddly enough, on this same day - a Monday - Abraham Lincoln was giving a similar type of speech in Peoria, Illinois, supporting the presidency of Zachary Taylor. The speech was similar in that it was an entertaining, out of the ordinary speech filled with "folderol." Lincoln likewise wanted to appear more homey and folksy than austere and over dignified.

Following is a brief newspaper report of Lincoln's appearance that same day (reported 3 days later).

Lincoln and J. Y. Scammon speak at courthouse in evening. After chairman "designated the spot where he should stand, Mr. L. blew his nose, bobbed his head, threw up his coat tail, and in the course of two hours was delivered of an immense amount of 'sound and fury'." He defends Taylor's seeming lack of principles and urges Free Soil men to support Taylor rather than Van Buren. (Source: Democratic Free Press October 11, 1848).

Naturally, Louis Napoleon ran for president the first chance he got. The office would be decided by a general election. On 20 December 1848 Louis Napoleon received approximately 5,400,000 votes for president to approximately 1,500,000 for his nearest competitor Monsieur Cavaignac - a landslide.

The improbability of this was astounding. Louis Napoleon could not get a single unpaid person to support him during his attempted coups at Strasbourg or at Boulogne and now all of a sudden he is awarded the presidency of France in a landslide election! Was this a case of satanic influence? Or was it massive tampering with the system of counting votes?

At this time, the beginnings of the Napoleon III cult had its origin. Note the sentiments of the people who supported Louis Napoleon and the effect his election to president had upon them.

> They realized that salvation could come
> only as the result of a forceful energy, an
> invincible firmness, and they know the Prince possesses
> these. That is why they have given him an overwhelming
> majority which exerted its full weight in the
> balance.

> If the Prince is proclaimed First Magistrate of the Republic, there is no doubt he will soon exchange that title for another the only one that is really suitable for him.

> It is dazzling, terrifying almost. By five million and a half votes the People has declared its will to have one man as its head. It desires him for chief. To-morrow it will demand him as master.

> December 20th. The weather is magnificent; "the sun of Austerlitz," say our friends as they meet. . . . And
> yet, never before did such suspense hold me by the throat like a hand of iron, as we wait for the results of the Presidential election ! (2 - et al)

Demand him as master! Yes, a terrifying thought that people should elevate a fellow human being to such heights, a fellow human being who only months before could not get a single person interested in putting his name on a ballot for a lowly deputy's position.

Now that Louis was president he immediately faced a major obstacle. According to the constitution, the president could only serve one four year term. The Emperor certainly could not abide by this. He required full, unfettered power.

But before tending to this, Louis had to solve another problem. He had to make certain that the proper pope - one he approved of - was firmly seated on the throne in Rome. The pope who Louis approved and was to rule for the next twenty years would be well known for his anti-Semitism and his strong dislike for democracy and individual freedoms.

Eventually, on April 12, 1850, Pope Pius returned to full power with Louis's help. Acting as an Emperor it was very important to have an ally in Rome.

## EMPEROR'S FIRST ACTS

Louis Napoleon had been in control as president for only a short time, and already there were factions growing against him. A great many people did not agree with his Italian policy and were prepared to wage violent opposition to it. But the president knew exactly how to suppress the will of his people and to make certain that free speech could not be heard in his domain.

What follows is a description of how one of the many protests in Paris against Louis Napoleon was brutally put down, called "working a rising." The man "working" the rising, Changarnier, was one of Louis's military hatchet men.

> This is how Changarnier "works" a rising. He allowed the column of 20,000 demonstrators (headed by Etienne Arago) to form itself; when the column marching down from the Boulevards, had reached the Madeleine, he debouched from the Rue de la Paix and cut it in two, driving back one portion towards the church and the other to the Porte Saint-Denis, sweeping the pavements with his cavalry and emptying the side streets with his infantry and municipal guards, who were led by the Commissaries of Police. This is how Changarnier uses His scalpel. (4)

At the same time that Louis was butchering his own people, a plague of cholera was sweeping over the city and killing many of the other citizens.

Louis Napoleon survived his first months through brute force. Now it was time for him to declare himself dictator, which would take even more brute force used over a great many more people.

Now being called "The Man of December" because of the important events that he undertook in December, the president got busy wiping at all of his internal opposition - like clockwork.

The Date was December 2, 1851. The man of December was to strike again and this time assume dictatorial powers over the country of France.

The entire affair was perfectly orchestrated. Louis wrote out exact instructions on how power was to be taken and gave these to the men in charge of carrying them out. It read something like a laundry list:

> From 3 to 4 a.m. reception of the Commissaries of
> Police by the Prefect, and instructions given to them.

> At 5.30 occupation of the buildings of the Assembly.

At 6 arrest of dangerous Generals, Representatives, heads of societies, and democrats.

At 6.30 posting up of proclamations, and disposition of troops near the houses where arrests are taking place.

At 7 everything ought to be completed.

At 8 the Minister of the Interior sends his instructions to the participants. (1)


Literally like a *thief in the night*, Louis Napoleon became dictator of France. Does this not mirror the biblical description of how the evil one would takeover the earth on the last days?

And upon directions of the Emperor, *the new world order* was to be set in place.

> It was not until two o'clock that the five men who were about to lay the foundations of a *new order of things* separated. (1)

Paris woke up the next morning to find that the Emperor had taken over, with silent terror.

> And this is what was seen on December 2nd. The population of Paris gazing, half-stupefied, at the walls covered with placards; troops collecting here and there; messengers galloping in all directions; arrests of all sorts taking place, including all the elements of danger, whether of those in high places, such as the Assembly, or those of lower position in the street leaders of secret societies, and men who had erected barricades, both moral and material.
>
> The clear and ringing language of the placards ran as follows:
>
> IN THE NAME OF THE FRENCH PEOPLE
>
> The President of the Republic decrees:
>
> Art. I. The National Assembly is dissolved.
>
> Art. IV. A State of Siege is decreed within the limits of the 1st Military Division. (4)

This is what the commoner saw: his city under siege. But the officials of the former government saw far worse. Each of them was visited by an officer and brutally placed under arrest. More than three hundred of them were immediately taken to prison, all rights stripped from them. Their only crime: they did not support Louis Napoleon as dictator.

A full 30,000 people were eventually caught in the dictator's purge.

Newspapers were immediately censored and all public gatherings forbidden. Recalling Louis's many quotes, this must have been how he would "give the people my heart."

The process of Louis's rise to dictatorship was very carefully planned. And it required a great deal of money to succeed. Where did this money come from?

Here is a most curious matter about this affair which few if any historians note. At the beginning of his rise to power, Louis essentially did not have any useful political backing. Somehow he had to establish a core of followers around him. The only way to do that was with money.

He had to pay armies of soldiers and "officials" to do his bidding, surrounding himself with a mercenary army which was loyal to him, not to France.

Where did this man who was previously very short of money suddenly acquire huge sums of gold to pay off accomplices and to buy the acquiescence of others?

**CREATING GOLD AND SPECIAL WEAPONS**

What you are about to read has been taken from completely unbiased sources. Not only are they unbiased but they are extremely conservative. What could be more conservative than a 19$^{th}$ century banking organization?

Where did Napoleon III get his money from? Had he found a way to produce gold, silver and other precious metals?

But, even on the smaller scale of walking around money, Napoleon's friends wondered where he even got so much of that.

> (...and I...) went over once more the measures we intended to take to carry the affair through quickly ... After which the Prince took from his desk a box which he opened, saying to Saint-Arnaud: 'Here is all my wealth, General; take the half of it. You will perhaps want some of it to-morrow, to distribute in presents.' The box contained sixty thousand francs; Saint-Arnaud accepted only ten thousand."

"These figures have been slightly misrepresented," said I with a smile.

"Yes, they talk of 500,000 francs given to Morny and the same amount to Saint-Arnaud, 100,000 to myself, and 50,000 to Espinasse. Where the deuce could the Prince have got that amount of gold?" (2)

It's important to note that these comments were made contemporaneously with the events of the coup. And they were made by men without any knowledge at the time of the suspicions that Louis Napoleon was the true Emperor. In fact, they were supporters of his.

Why is this at all important? Because it's another one of the very many clues that point toward Napoleon III as having access to extraordinary powers. The Emperor would have access to immense amounts of gold which would have been acquired through out-of-the-ordinary means with the assistance of his infernal patron Major Frazer.

The following report is of *immense importance*. It was made by one of the largest banking oversight agencies in Europe during the mid 19th century. By its very nature it is a highly conservative organization. However, the following report about Napoleon III's apparent production of gold is nothing less than astounding! It is given here in totality due to its exceptional importance.

The following paragraph from the Bankers' Reporter additionally testifies to the existence of some mysterious source from which Napoleon obtained gold and silver:

"It has been a great mystery to English bankers and to the Directors of the Bank of England, how the bullion of the Bank of Franco could be so greatly increased within the last three years, while the institution has been constantly sending gold to England, to Germany, and to America, Not long since the Bank of France drew some fifteen million francs in silver from the Bank of England, which it paid for in gold bars with the French mint stamp on them. At its last report it showed a balance of one hundred and seventeen million francs in gold, while the amount one year ago was under eighty million nearly one third increase. **It is whispered that this abundance of gold is the result of a scientific discovery, which the Emperor Napoleon has secured the monopoly of. Gold is at the present moment manufactured at Paris in a secret manner.** Though it is not known how extensively the precious metal is produced, yet several hundred-weight of the material were taken to a certain place on the first of each month. **Everything is conducted with the utmost secrecy.** None of the workmen are allowed to leave, and nothing definite can be known; but the fact that gold is produced is beyond peradventure. How long Napoleon III. will be able to keep this wonderful secret remains to be seen." (Special report as noted)

The report is detailing a clandestine gold-making operation under the control of the government of France which is directly overseen by Napoleon III. As suggested, if gold could be produced so could weapons of immense destructive force.

And there isn't any doubt that the ability to formulate such a device could be found in the writings of such great men as Sardi Canot who attempted to construct a machine that was powered by a mysterious energy force in 1824. There is also Pierre and Mari Currie, LaPlace, and many other great French scientific minds of the 19$^{th}$ century.

I am not suggesting that France under the Emperor was on the threshold of creating a full-fledged nuclear missile arsenal. But it is very possible that they could have been experimenting with nuclear explosive cannon shot or other more contemporary forms of delivery.

There was only one thing missing. A man of genius who could coordinate it all and provide the final expertise.

Would that have been the goal of Major Frazer?

Curiously, this is the only description of Major Frazer that is known to exist, and even that in itself is enlightening. It here follows:

> Major Frazer. "This Frazer is a curious and mysterious man about whom everybody speaks in a whisper, with significant gestures and ambiguous smiles. No one knows exactly who he is or what he does, yet he has some distinguished relations, such as M. de Hubner, the Austrian Ambassador, and that Mme Boscari de Villeplane at whose house I have occasionally met him. They say he is a deserter, a spy, and I don't know what else. He belongs to no country. His great-grandfather was a Scotsman. His father married and settled at Lisbon. His sisters are married to Italian marquises. He himself was born in Portugal. He was in Russia while still a young man and was admitted to the cadet corps. He was present at the Battle of Leipzig, and returned to Paris with the Russian army. Since 1827 he has been a Parisian and eccentric. He lives between Tortoni's and the Cafe de Foy, in a room furnished with an iron bedstead, a bearskin, a collection of boots, and a cask of Cyprus wine.
>
> He belongs to quite a number of social sets, and yet he does not play. He speaks all the languages there are, can recite six odes of Horace straight off, goes the pace with M. de Musset, holds debates in Latin with M. Jules Janin, and is interested in economics. A most accomplished man. (1)

One very lengthy paragraph and one very short paragraph. And thereby is an entire biography found between the lines.

It is clear what this description is actually saying. Major Frazer is some type of extraordinary being living quietly yet brilliantly amongst the common mortal population.

His appearance in the story about Lincoln and the Emperor is a brief one but with extreme significance.

## LINCOLN ELECTED PRESIDENT

After devoting himself to his legal profession for a decade, Lincoln ran for president as the head of his own newly formed Republican Party and won.

The raw statistics of Lincoln's law practice over a 23 year period reveal that he took part in over 5,100 cases in Illinois and that he and his partners appeared before the Illinois Supreme Court on more than 400 occasions.

During Lincoln's practice it is estimated that he would have averaged at least one case before the court a day, many of them mere filings, of course, but this was in any respect an enormous workload.

So, why did he return to politics and why in particular did he run for president? Maybe it was the following remark he made when he was a young man delivering produce for his store to Southern merchants and he saw slaves being sold:

"Boys, if I ever get a chance to hit slavery, by God I'll hit it hard!"

In 1854 Lincoln had a chance to regain his seat in the Illinois Legislature, but he turned that down in favor of running as a Republican for a place in the U.S. Congress. Although he did not win the national seat he came very close to winning the Republican nomination for vice president in 1856.

The year 1858 was when Lincoln participated in his famous debates with Douglas. It was during one of the debates that Lincoln's immortal words, "A house divided against itself cannot stand," were spoken in Peoria, Illinois.

Lincoln was defeated in the battle at the poles with Douglas, but a great victory was to come from it in just two years. His brilliance, friendliness and wit during the debates had won him great respect. Then came the Republican nomination for president in 1860.

Abraham Lincoln won the election for president as a Republican by defeating the Democrat Stephen Douglas, the

Southern Democrat John C. Breckinridge, and John Bell who ran for the just created Constitutional Union Party.

While Lincoln did not do well in the popular vote, he won a large majority in the Electoral College.

The War Between the States began with his election as seven Southern states immediately seceded. The rest would soon follow. And another continent would be brutalized by war.

But Lincoln was to find that HIS war would extend across the Atlantic and against a foe unlike any he was facing in America.

## EMPEROR NAPOLEON III

The Emperor was dictator of France, but he was still not satisfied. He wanted even more power. According to him, he owed it to his country. France was waiting for his absolute domination.

> "Yes, all France is possessed by the fever of Empire. Yes, Louis Napoleon is a Man of Providence."

On November 21, 1852 Louis Napoleon proclaimed himself emperor of France, naming himself Napoleon III, after a "vote" was taken and the people acclaimed him emperor. Who actually voted and how these "votes" were counted is never divulged.

The Emperor was in absolute control of France. His next goal was the world, including the United States of America which, at this point, was still not under the protection of Abraham Lincoln.

But the new emperor needed more experience in actual warfare so he took his next adventure.

One of the main goals of the Emperor was to plunge the world into chaos. Of course, amongst the more certain ways to do this is by causing and spreading wars at which Louis Napoleon was a master.

His first attempt at causing chaos and mass murder by re-seating the pope on the throne of Rome was a huge success. Death and suffering had been widespread, and thousands of people had been confined to prison.

The pope had his own secret police force similar to the KGB who went door to door arresting people who were opposed to his rule or who were considered heretics. Because torture was generally frowned upon, this pope used incarceration as his most potent weapon. He would simply have his enemies locked in a dark, miserable dungeon where they remained until they died or were eventually liberated.

The next object of mayhem would be the Crimea. This was a war poised to happen, and Napoleon III was ready to instigate the disaster.

Russia was at the centre of the problem. Tsar Nicholas wanted to carve up the Ottoman province of Turkey between Russia and England. With this plan in mind, in June of 1853 the Russian army invaded the Turkish provinces of Wallachia and Moldavia.

Wallachia had been the former principality ruled by Vlad the Impaler, more commonly known as Dracula. It seems fitting that the Emperor would have dealings with this area of the world.

There is a supernatural event worth noting in conjunction with the Crimean War. One evening Napoleon III and some friends were entertaining themselves with demonstrations of mediumistic hypnotism. During the course of events, the subject of the death of a prominent party to the war came up. This is how it transpired as recorded by Baron D'Ambes.

It happened last year at the Tuileries,
where the Empress was entertaining some privileged
friends. After dinner there was an exhibition of
hypnotism. The hypnotist proposed to send one of the
company into the hypnotic sleep. Lots were drawn, and
the Prince de la Tour d'Auvergne was chose. He was
put to sleep, and questions were asked of him, which he
answered.

"What do you see on the horizon?"

"Armies meeting in battle with great bloodshed.
Look, there is the Officer in command. He is pale."

The Emperor, much disturbed, came forward and put
Questions.

"Will he return?"

"No."

"Will he be wounded?"

"No."

"Killed?"

"No, neither; but he will die. I see him distinctly.

He is on horseback; his face shows traces of suffering. No human power will save him from that disease."
The prediction came true.

March 2nd. "The newspapers publish this dispatch: The Emperor Nicholas is dead."

Nobody had the slightest expectation of such an event.

The imposing stature of Nicholas…offered no suggestion of so sudden an end. I had seen him in St. Petersburg.

I am told that he succumbed to an affection of the lungs which had threatened him for some time. His death had been predicted two years ago by spiritualism. Some Russian ladies told me the circumstance. At a Spiritualistic séance somebody had indiscreetly asked of the turning table how long the Tsar would live. This was in 1853; and the answer was two knocks.(2)

The major area of contention of the Crimean War was the formidable naval station of the Russians' at Sebastopol. It came under an eleven month assault by the allied forces of England, France and the Piedmont.

The Russian forces were finally overrun at Sebastopol on September 20, 1855. The war, however, did not officially end until October 25 with the famous charge of the Light Brigade on the seaport of Balaklava. And even that charge was made on fallacious orders.

One of the primary purposes of this war was for the glory of France. Glory! Yes, glory. It was believed that such a great victory would restore the lost glory to the new French empire.

The Crimean war was one of the most hideous of wars when considering the amount of pure suffering it caused. Soldiers on all sides died by the thousands upon thousands not from the sudden merciless sting of a bullet or a cannon shell exploding but by the slow, miserable, agonizing death brought about by dysentery. The other soldiers died either by freezing to death or from starvation or from other diseases. Although thousands were killed in battle, the thousands who died either sick or frozen on the cold ground were even more!

And it has been said that France did not even garner any glory from the dismal affair. Napoleon III was very disappointed. But the Emperor had certainly done his job. And there was much more to come both in Europe and the United States.

Consider what Abraham Lincoln was about to face. The War Between the States was going to be worse than the Crimean War because it was to last even longer.

The loss of only one man - on either side - caused Lincoln great anguish. The loss of thousands were barely noticed by Napoleon III and Nicholas. They cared only for their own glory.

I rely on the great Victor Hugo for this description of the true Napoleon III, murderer of the innocent:

> The man who kills, transports, exiles, expels, proscribes, plunders, this man with languid gesture, with glassy eye, who walks with a preoccupied air in the midst of the horrible thing which he has done like a sort of sinister somnambulist. They said of Louis Bonaparte, perhaps with a good, perhaps with an evil meaning, for these beings have strange flatterers: "He is a dictator, he is a despot, nothing more." (4)

A word should be mentioned about Victor Hugo. He was an ardent supporter of Louis Napoleon at the beginning of his reign; he even wrote a book in praise of him.

Then Hugo realized that all of the propaganda spewing from Napoleon's camp was nothing more than that - empty propaganda. The problem is there is a vast amount of this propaganda filling textbooks and history books throughout the world. Items written in praise of this madman Louis Napoleon are lies!

Below is only a tiny list of the lies in bulk that were part of Napoleon III's self-created glory.

> "The Empire is peace." He said often while destroying all foes. "Napoleon gave his brothers to the nations of Europe; for my part I should wish to give them my heart."(1)

Did he tell that to the citizens that were being massacred in the streets who were protesting the French invasion of Italy?

> "My dear D'Ambes, I often think of the… which society owes to the unfortunate the disinherited, and the more I reflect on this the more I am convinced that there is still much to be done in this direction. If I should one day win power, I shall not fail to employ it in making good the deficiencies on this point." (1)

Apparently he forget about the woman he impregnated while imprisoned at Ham and eventually left her and her child in a destitute position. Yes, a man of glorious WORDS.

In the same year that Lincoln was debating Douglas in the world's only existing democracy, the Emperor determined that the glory of his empire needed a little more polish.

Thus, in 1858 Napoleon III mounted a naval expedition that sailed half way across the world to Indochina. He sent a large force to the small country of Viet Nam for the purpose of punishing its leadership for mistreating the Catholic missionaries who had been dispatched to this country to "civilize" it.

The people of Viet Nam waged a stronger defense of their home than expected so the mighty emperor declared total war against this Southeast Asian country. He sent more ships and more troops and beat the tiny country into submission. Not only was France the master of Viet Nam but the defeated country was forced to pay its master an indemnity for a war it did not start.

After pouncing on Viet Nam, the emperor turned toward Cambodia and subdued it as well, eventually turning it into a French Protectorate.

Apparently the emperor had not gained enough glory and during the 1860's sent forces into Japan, Korea and China. These ventures were moderately successful, winning large indemnities as a reward for the effort.

In 1859 Napoleon III returned to Italy. This time he was determined to rid the country of the Austrian influence, at least from the entire northern part of Italy, which he did. Napoleon III continued to protect his friend Pope Pius IX, keeping French forces in Rome itself, protecting the pope from attack and/or ouster by the new Italian government.

This might be a good time to recall one of Napoleon III's most famous quotes: **"The Empire means peace."** Apparently his understanding of the meaning of the word peace was quite different from most people. This concept will be visited again when Napoleon III looks back on his reign of peace.

At any rate, Napoleon would shortly resume better terms with the Germanic world during the Mexican revolution when he would set up a Hapsburg on the throne of Mexico. And this will bring him into direct confrontation with Abraham Lincoln who was then reaching the height of his political genius.

## ASSASSINATING THE EMPEROR

For a man who claimed to be greatly loved by his people, Napoleon III was the target of an exceptional number of assassination attempts.

There was a general hatred directed at Napoleon III by a large segment of the population of Europe, not only of France. Every relative of every person whom he consigned to the hellhole which was Devil's Island would surely want to see this mad Emperor dead!

But it was beginning to seem as though he possessed godlike invincibility. He seemed to have miraculously escaped many attempts made on his life. On April 28, 1855 while Emperor Napoleon was riding down the street he stopped as a pedestrian approached him. The man was reaching into his pocket for something and Napoleon III thought he was about to withdraw a petition to give him.

He withdrew a pistol instead and fired at the Emperor at point blank range. Yet he missed! There was not any misfiring of the weapon, nor did anyone jostle the man in anyway. He simply fired at Louis Napoleon at point blank range and missed!

The would-be assassin was arrested and sentenced to be executed but the punishment was commuted.

Even the Emperor recognized his escape from certain death, and remarked, "I have not the slightest fear of attacks of assassins. There are lives which exist simply as instruments of the decrees of God. As long as my task is unfinished, I have no danger to fear." If Louis Napoleon had interchanged the word Devil for God he would have been more correct.

There were several more casual attempts on the life of Napoleon III, mostly by people firing upon him randomly from crowds. This happened a lot because he was well hated rather than well loved. One of the attempts was made as Louis was about to enter the Theatre Italian and in this case the culprit named Delmare was apprehended.

It should here be noted the irony of how both Lincoln and Napoleon III were hunted down in and around theatres.

Another attempt on the Emperor's life which seemed to have been repulsed by divine (or infernal) providence also occurred outside of an opera house. A bomb had been set to explode in the street at the time that the emperor's carriage was passing. The explosion was horrific and killed many bystanders.

General Roguet had been sitting directly across from Louis and was gravely wounded. So too were three footmen and twelve lancers who formed the escort guard. Even one of the unfortunate horses was killed.

But Napoleon III and the empress escaped with only cuts and bruises. These deliverances from death served to inspire the cult of the divine emperor. This was a real and an active cult with "chapters" throughout Europe.

A man named Andrew Towianski founded a sect in Europe based on the worship of Napoleon I. This sect spread throughout the world and its rituals and ceremonies were performed in the strictest secrecy. Each member of this sect possessed a picture of Napoleon I rising from his grave with a halo around his head.

A central feature of this cult was belief in metempsychosis which is an expectation that the spirit of Napoleon I would be resuscitated in the body of his nephew Napoleon III, so that they would in reality be one and the same person.

The adherents to this sect openly referred to Napoleon as their saviour, and they even re-invented the Lord's Prayer so that it referred to Louis Napoleon. It started thusly: "Our prince who art in power, they kingdom come, thy will be done at home as it is abroad..." One of the "priests" of this cult was known to frequently say, "God created Bonaparte and rested from his labours."

Napoleon III was aware of these cults and his deification. A friend of his once told him, "Some think you are an angel, Sire: some a devil: but all agree you are more than a man."

An Irish Bishop named Talbot told Lord John Russell that he knew for a fact that Napoleon III had sold himself to the devil and consulted with him as to his policy. Bishop Talbot was a close confidante of Pope Pius IX. What if this were actually true!

Who could stand against Emperor Napoleon III?

## LINCOLN PREPARES FOR BATTLE

The Civil War had begun on April 12, 1861 with the Confederate Army opening fire on Fort Sumter in Charleston Harbor, South Carolina. Full scale hostilities commenced and for the first couple of years the war effort went badly for the North. The South continued to win major battle after major battle and this caused the nations of Europe to consider recognizing the Confederacy as a sovereign state.

The three primary countries interested in the outcome of the War Between the States were England, Russia and France. Not only were they considering recognizing the South, they were also considering stepping in and negotiating a settlement or more. The United States had become an important trading partner with these countries, and now shortages of necessities were beginning to appear in Europe, particularly cotton.

Any type of negotiations, of course, would require that the Confederacy be recognized as an independent state with the right to negotiate its future. After the many early defeats the North suffered, many northerners were beginning to favor just such a tactic. They were growing tired of a war they had expected to win within a few weeks. A negotiated settlement was very appealing to many people.

Lincoln was in a literal sense fighting the world. The Union - the American Republic - was despised by the monarchies because of the democracy inherent in it. They could not abide freedom for the common citizen. Neither could the pope, who was political ruler of the Papal States and religious ruler of millions of Catholics throughout the world. And he was now infallible!

Even England favored the South. According to Prime Minister Gladstone, "Jefferson Davis had made a nation" and that the restoration of the Union could not be accomplished by force. The Marquis of Salisbury stated, "The people of the South are the natural allies of England."

Pope Pius IX had this to say on the matter:

There can be no doubt in any sound mind that the North and the South require a different government. The conservative elements of Southern society would be in too small a minority to control the aggressiveness of the wild and wanton democracy, which is found ever and anon to seize the reins of government at the North, under the most propitious circumstances. (Papal letter)

There were three main reasons why the pope hated Lincoln. One reason was that Lincoln was a supporter of the temperance idea and the pope owned hundreds of acres of vineyards. He had a great many customers to lose in the United States if the American President chose to make alcohol illegal.

Another reason is that Lincoln was clearly anti-slavery and the pope favored slavery.

And the third reason: cologne. Cologne? Yes, the pope manufactured a special cologne bearing his mark and since one of the ingredients in this cologne is alcohol he stood to lose that concession to Catholics in America as well.

There actually was a fourth reason for the pope's hatred of Lincoln. It was because the pope was the ally of the Emperor and the American president was their adversary on that specific ground.

Pope Pius IX actively supported the Confederate cause and was an admirer of Jefferson Davis. He even sent a personal letter to the President of the Confederacy, along with a photograph. The letter in full follows.

Salutations:

We have just received with all suitable welcome the persons sent by you to place in our hands your letter, dated the 23rd of September last. Not slight was the pleasure we experienced when we learned, from those persons and the letter, with what feelings of joy and gratitude, you were animated, *illustrious and honourable President*, as soon as you were informed of our letters to our venerable brother, John, Archbishop of New York, and John Archbishop of New Orleans, dated the 18th of October of last year, and in which we have with all our strength exerted and exhorted those venerable brothers that in their episcopal piety and solicitude, they should endeavor, with the most ardent zeal, and in our name to bring about the end of that fatal civil war which has broken out in *those countries* in order that the American people may obtain peace and concord and dwell charitably together. It is particularly agreeable to us that your *illustrious and honourable President*, and your people, were animated with the same desires of peace and tranquillity which we have in our letters inculcated upon our venerable brothers. May it please God at the same time to make the other peoples of America and their rulers, reflecting seriously how terrible is civil war, and what calamities it engenders, listen to inspirations of a calmer spirit and adopt resolutely the part of peace. As for us, we shall not cease

(Signed) Pius IXth.

---

## WORLDWIDE SLAVERY

Why should anyone in Europe care about slavery? Because there is more than one form of slavery and the old European system which was still in use was built upon these "soft" forms of slavery.

This would included the so-called "forced labor" which was made up of people who were either debtors, prisoners, political enemies or any number of classifications of people who were on the bottom of society.

It would also include those conscripted into the army of which there were hundreds of thousands if not millions.

And of course there were all of those people who worked the plantations for their European colonial masters.

If Lincoln could force an end to slavery in America, the European leaders - who were kings and other nobles - were terrified that it would affect their way of life, too.

As you can see, Lincoln versus Napoleon III truly was a confrontation of worldwide significance and it would be fought both on paper and on the southern border of the United States which at that time was the Confederacy.

Does this not seem a little bit like Armageddon? The entire world lined up against the Union with Abraham Lincoln as the one great defender standing up against them all. This is not an over dramatization. Lincoln truly stood **ALONE** in his steadfast determination to save the Union at all costs! At all costs!

The major nations of Europe were not only debating whether or not to recognize the Confederacy but whether or not they should actively step in and force negotiations to take place. Again, before this could happen the Confederacy would have to be recognized as a sovereign state.

The government of Jefferson Davis was attempting to force the issue by sending a delegation to England to discuss such a proposal. They were intercepted in the process in an act of blatant piracy under the auspices of the government of Abraham Lincoln.

The two Confederate commissioners dispatched to Europe, Mason and Slidell, were forcibly detained on November 8, 1861 by an armed U.S. ship while they were sailing aboard a British steamer. Captain Wilkes of the U.S. Navy had the two men removed from the British ship, taken aboard the American vessel and sailed back in custody to the Port of Boston. They were placed in confinement at Fort Warren.

The only way war was averted with Great Britain was by the issuance of a politically perfect reply to the British Government: "The . . . persons in question are now held in military custody at Fort Warren, in the State of Massachusetts. They will be cheerfully liberated. Your lordship will please indicate a time and place for receiving them."

The Lincoln administration knew that this "generous" offer would not be accepted by the government of Great Britain. The government of Great Britain had no interest in receiving these individuals anywhere at any time. Thus the matter was closed.

The point of this is to demonstrate the great detriment it was <u>not to have</u> official recognition as a sovereign country. The commission sent by the Confederate States did not have any political standing other than as members of a hostile force waging war against an already existing valid government - The Union.

This did not prevent the South from sending other representatives to Great Britain. One particular contingent was near to concluding an agreement on a large loan to be taken out by the Confederacy when a great disaster befell the South.

## THE EMPEROR ATTACKS AMERICA

Napoleon III was already ravaging most of Europe. He had spread his assault into the Mideast where he took possession of the Holy Places. Napoleon III also conquered Syria, Algeria and other portions of the African Continent. Chaos was rampant across the globe. Again, does this not seem like Armageddon?

Not only did Napoleon III conquer any country that stood in his path, he was brutal in his methods. It didn't matter if his opponent was fighting with only spears and shields, the outcome was all that mattered. Napoleon was pleased when the other side was utterly decimated.

What follows is a description of the manner in which Napoleon III desired war to be carried out. Described is an attack by French troops on a tribe of nearly helpless Arabs who had sought refuge in a cave.

The following barbarous carnage will be presented in full to further convince the reader of the true depths of Napoleon III's evil.

> Pelissier dictated terms to them, which they considered too hard. They returned to their refuge, declaring that they preferred to die with their wives and children. The fire was relit. It burned the whole of the day and far into the night. The cries of the Arabs were frightful, and the troops had orders to give no
>
> quarter. A column of flame rose, raging and terrible, from the cave. On the morning of the 20th no voice was to be heard, and nothing was visible but a glowing mass. It was decided to examine the interior of the cave when the fire had burnt itself out. The scene was beyond description. Horses and camels, seized with madness, had, in their efforts to escape, trodden and
>
> mangled whatever came in their way. Men and women were lying in heaps, suffocated ; some were burnt to a

cinder. The men had to climb over corpses to make a way for themselves. They found more than a thousand. Some of the wretched creatures still breathed. At the back of the cave, bodies were found pressed hard standing upright as they were, against the rifts, in the

effort to avoid suffocation. There were some sixty Arabs still alive, but when they were brought into the open air they expired immediately. Others had been crushed under masses of rock detached by the heat. Many grasped scimitars in their hands; and many bore signs of terrible wounds which they had inflicted upon one another in vain efforts to escape. (2)

The United States was tearing itself apart with the War Between the States and The Emperor was ready to assault the New World with exactly the same type of ferocity and cruelty.

Mexico was to become the next target. It owed a great deal of money to Britain, Spain and France. The three countries joined together and sent an armed force to Mexico in order to collect the funds due them. Because of the Mexican-American War the Treasury of Mexico was bankrupt which was why President Benito Juarez stopped making payments.

The representatives of Spain and Great Britain made arrangements with the government of Mexico and then departed.

Napoleon III's forces remained. He had much more than collection of war debts in mind. He planned to "collect" the entire country and beyond.

But it wouldn't be as easy as he apparently thought it would be. Napoleon's early attack on Mexico was not highly successful. He had expected to be greeted as some form of liberator with the clergy in the forefront tossing magnolia blossoms in his direction. It didn't happen that way.

On May 5, 1862 (later to be celebrated as Conci de Mayo) a combined force of French and Mexican troops were led by General Lorenz toward Puebla, Mexico. The town was defended by Texas-born General Ignacio Zaragoza with a small force of soldiers and bands of independence-loving Native Americans with machetes.

When the French tried to charge with their cavalry they were countered by herds of stampeding cattle that had been driven by the Indians into the battlefield which had been made a quagmire by a heavy rain the day before.

Not only were the French denied another massacre, but they were soundly defeated and they made an ignominious retreat.

It wasn't until two years later that the French were able to bring in a large number of reinforcements to realize their conquest of Mexico. Prince Maximilian of the Hapsburg Dynasty was destined to be crowned Emperor of Mexico.

On April 14, 1864 (note how many disastrous things occur on April 14th) Maximilian boarded the frigate Novara and sailed directly to Rome first.

Here he received the blessings of Pope Pius IX who by this act was clearly made a part of the unholy alliance with the Emperor. After receiving the pope's approval, Maximilian left for the New World, arriving at Vera Cruz on May 28, 1864.

He then proceeded to Cordova and Orizaba where 10,000 of the native "Indians" acclaimed his sovereignty.

On June 5th Maximilian marched into Puebla, and, at the site of a dismal defeat of the French-led forces in 1862, overran the Mexican army. Then on the 12th of the same month he claimed Mexico City as his own with a contingent of the huge French army supporting him!

The French army was poised on the southern border of the Confederacy/United States. One of the primary reasons they did not cross the border to join forces with the Confederacy and attack the Union is because the Mexican Brigadier General Porfiro Diaz had set up a provisional government in the north of Mexico with a large loyalist army defending the area.

In a very real sense the United States as it exists today is greatly indebted to General Diaz. He held the French at bay just long enough.

Abraham Lincoln had been closely watching the situation in Mexico from the start. In fact, he had been observing it since the Mexican-American War. He knew that his opposition to that war had been correct because the results of it were now showing themselves. Mexico had been made such a weakened country it had become open to outside invasion.

It was not by mere chance that simultaneously with the start of the War Between the States that Napoleon III invaded Mexico with an expeditionary force.

A crucial event in history took place early in the French-Mexican campaign which has not received high recognition from historians. President Lincoln unofficially received a visitor from the Napoleon family at the White House.

Lincoln was fully aware of Napoleon III's desire for world domination and could deduce the plans he had for America. He was most likely aware that Napoleon III was widely believed to be the Anti-Christ by many. The visitor to the Lincoln White House was a cousin of Napoleon III's who was familiarly called "Plon" but was more commonly addressed as Prince Napoleon.

His visit to the White House was a semi-diplomatic one without any true authority vested in him. It would best be termed a "feeling out" of the American President. What follows is a description of the meeting, written by Camille Ferri Pisani.

"Our meeting was not so gay. The President shook our hands, after sharing the Prince's. I feared, for a moment, that the interview would end with this silent demonstration. Mr. Lincoln gained a few more minutes by asking the Prince to sit down and by sitting himself, the whole affair being done with a great moving of chairs. But, once these new positions were acquired, the two parties sat opposite each other silently, without troubling to go any further. The Prince, impatient because he had to wait, took a cruel pleasure in remaining silent. Finally, the President took the risk of speaking of Prince Lucien, his father. Mr. Lincoln was on the wrong track and he was warned [Prince Napoleon was **Jerome Napoleon**'s son, not Lucien's.] This incident made him lose his confidence, still further. A few words were then exchanged on the rain, the weather and our crossing. The Prince still maintained his polite but cold front—as he customarily does when he does not care to help the conversation. Finally, Mr. Lincoln once more resorted to the handshaking; as we were seven on our side, and they were two on the other, the ceremony lasted long enough so that we soon reached the time limit usually assigned to this kind of meeting. Everyone retired, glad to have completed the official presentation, for these customs are generally boring, and their annoyance is only compensated by the hope for the more intimate and interesting relationships of which they are the necessary prelude. (Memoirs of Camille Ferri Pisani)

It is doubtful that Lincoln's seeming rudeness was accidental. It was a message of contempt to the Napoleons and most likely a true sign of an unwillingness to deal with emissaries of the Emperor.

Why should Lincoln not be rude to the relative of a man who was threatening to destroy the Union which he was so desperately trying to save and who had blatantly defied the Monroe

Doctrine? The visit itself by Prince Napoleon was a tactless gesture - an affront.

Lincoln's reaction revealed his complete understanding of the politics of the world and the morass that had been created by the vainglory of the madman Napoleon III.

## LINCOLN QUESTIONS THE SPIRITS

Many examples of Louis Napoleon's ties with the supernatural have been cited. Abraham Lincoln is also well known for his interest in the supernatural. Some have claimed that he was a natural medium. It is difficult to deny that he was in close touch with higher powers.

Lincoln's views on the eradication of slavery touched on the metaphysical. He did not believe it was a problem that could be solved by warfare. According to the president, "Whenever this question shall be settled, it must be settled on some philosophical basis."

There were claims that Lincoln was a spiritualist. Some say that this notion is ludicrous. Others, not. Maybe there was a middle ground. Lincoln clearly was a man of deep moral beliefs and strong philosophical leanings. He found himself in a logical dilemma for which he would use even unorthodox means to extricate himself.

At the centre of his internal struggles was the problem of slavery. According to him, "If slavery is not wrong, nothing is wrong." Yet, at the same time he was not an abolitionist - he was not willing to simply stamp out slavery once and for all. This was his struggle, pitting these two opposing beliefs against each other.

Lincoln seemed almost constantly to be anguishing over slavery. Note the following remarks.

"Slavery is founded in the selfishness of man's nature - opposition to it, in his love of justice."

"No man is good enough to govern another man without that other's consent."

"When Southern people tell us they are no more responsible for the origin of slavery than we are, I acknowledge the fact."

"Those who deny freedom to others, deserve it not for themselves; and under a just God, cannot long retain it."

The question might be asked as to whether or not he truly believed what he sometimes espoused; that slavery was only of secondary importance in regards to the War Between the States.

It is clear what Abraham Lincoln personally thought about slavery. What is unclear is how he could maintain such contradictory opinions for so long without making an ultimate decision - **free the slaves**.

Lincoln continued to claim that the primary reason for fighting the War Between the States was to maintain the Union and not about slavery. But the reason that the two sides were fighting was due to the existence of slavery! Lincoln was caught in his own circular argument which is why it was so difficult for him to reach a definitive answer.

The president needed help to disentangle his thoughts on this subject. At some level he realized this. That is why, as a truly last resort, he turned to requesting the advice of a prominent spiritualist who offered to assist him through spirit intervention.

The process originally began when a close friend of Lincoln's named Thomas Richmond, contacted the sitting president about matters spiritualistic. Mister Richmond was a senator and an important businessman in the grain and shipping industries. He had written several letters while under trance which gave predictions for the future, including the war and slavery. He sent these to the president who read them with interest. And this seemed to open his mind to the possibility of seeking advice from the spirit world.

This introductory to spiritualism allowed for the deeper investigation into the subject that followed. A certain group of spiritualists, led by Nettie Colburn (later Henrietta Maynard) eventually won entrance into the White House for the purpose of supplying the president with information from the spirit world.

What follows is taken from the book, *"Was Abraham Lincoln A Spiritualist?"* written by Henrietta Maynard.

The opening passage concerns the president's first meeting with the group of spiritualists in the White House.

Mrs. Lincoln was talking with us in a pleasant strain (of music) when suddenly Mrs. Miller's hands fell upon the keys with a force that betokened a master hand, and the strains of a grand march filled the room. As the measured notes rose and fell we became silent. The heavy end of the piano began rising and falling in perfect time to the music. All at once it ceased and Mr. Lincoln stood upon the threshold of the room. (He afterwards informed us that the first notes of the music fell upon his ears as he reached the head of the grand staircase to descend, and that he kept step to the music until he reached the doorway).

Mr and Mrs. Laurie and Mrs. Miller were duly presented. Then I was led forward and presented. He stood before me, tall and kindly, with a smile on his face. Dropping his hand upon my head, he said, in a humorous tone, "So this is our 'little Nettie' is it, that we have heard so much about?" I could only smile and say, "Yes, sir," like any school girl; when he kindly led me to an ottoman. Sitting down in a chair, the ottoman at his feet, he began asking me questions in a kindly way about my mediumship; and I think he must have thought me stupid, as my answers were little beyond "Yes" and "No".

For more that an hour I was made to talk to him, and I learned from my friends afterward that it was upon matters that he seemed to fully understand, while they comprehended very little until that portion was reached that related to the forthcoming Emancipation Proclamation. He was charged with the utmost solemnity and force of manner not to abate the terms of its issue, and not to delay its enforcement as a law beyond the opening of the year; and he was assured that it was to be the *crowning event of his administration and life;* and that while he was counselled by strong parties to defer enforcement of it, hoping to supplant it by other measures and to delay action, *he must in no wise heed such counsel, but stand firm to his convictions and fearlessly perform the work and fulfil the mission for which he had been raised up by an overruling Providence.*

Mr. Somes said, "Mr. President, would it be improper for me to inquire whether there has been any pressure brought to bear upon you to defer the enforcement of the Proclamation?" To which the President replied: "Under these circumstances that question is perfectly proper, as we are all friends [smiling upon the company]. *It is taking all my nerve and strength to withstand such a pressure."*

Some of this pressure being wielded against Lincoln came from members of his administration who were hoping for a negotiated settlement with the Confederacy. Any settlement would necessarily have to include the continued existence of slavery in the South.

These forces were both real and anticipated. Lincoln knew of the men who were already outspoken against the emancipation of the slaves. But the unseen, unnamed foes may have been ever more threatening.

These foes were people like Horace Greeley. Horace Greeley was an immensely powerful man who, after the Emancipation Proclamation had been announced, attempted to force Lincoln to resign and to place General Rosencrans at the head of the Union Army and Vice President Hamlin in the president's position.

Lincoln was already anticipating the withdrawal of his name for re-election for the presidency before issuing the proclamation. He probably even anticipated the huge numbers of deserters from the Union Army who, while eager to fight for the Union as a cause, were not willing to die so that slaves could be viewed as their equals.

Indeed, these were formidable weights looming over Lincoln about to slam down upon him and crush him into oblivion.

Yet, he finally realized that it must be done! The issuance of the Emancipation Proclamation was the critical crisis point for Abraham Lincoln. He risked absolutely EVERYTHING by pronouncing it to the world. Even the war. It was possible that his entire army would mutiny.

This would delight the many European nations who were eager to broker a settlement between the two combatants or to attack the United States and carve it up for themselves.

Lincoln may not have been aware that in fact he held the weight of slavery for the entire world on his own shoulders. This was not just a fight against slavery in the United States, but the final results would affect the whole world. In a real sense America was going to set the standard for the rest of the planet.

During the séance held at the White House, it is claimed that Abraham Lincoln was indeed given a direct message from a combined consortium of spirits. The message was: "This Civil War will never cease. The shout of victory will never ring through the North, till you issue a proclamation that shall set free the enslaved millions of your unhappy country."

Did this message cause Abraham Lincoln to announce the proclamation? No one knows for certain. But it is a fact that it was only weeks after this séance that the proclamation was made official.

Abraham Lincoln finished writing the Emancipation Proclamation on September 22, 1862. He announced it to the world on January 1, 1863 and this was the date on which it took effect. This was the act which truly brought the War Between the States to an end! Not only did it place the Union on a firm moral ground without equivocation but it put an end to the world's interference in this country's national problem.

As long as the war was being fought simply to save the Union, the European powers were eager not only to attempt to oversee a truce between the warring sides but they also saw an opportunity of invading either the Confederacy, The Union or both. The European powers certainly could have joined together in such an endeavour.

However, when Lincoln declared that this war was about the abolition of slavery there were few European countries that wanted to interfere with such a cause. It would have been politically difficult to defend. Additionally, and most importantly, once Lincoln pronounced the Emancipation Proclamation there could not be ANY negotiating between North and South. And since slavery was the main issue of the war it would have been the only negotiating point.

Lincoln finally very clearly understood this, noting that the proclamation would be, "potent to prevent foreign intervention."

Great Britain and most of the other countries in Europe at this point relented. It wasn't just the proclamation that brought a halt to any attempts to negotiate a settlement but the fact that the Union had just won a major victory at Antietam. The Confederacy would soon be in desperate condition.

Pope Pius IX, however, still favoured the Confederate cause, stating that the Union's only cause was to dominate and punish the South. The pope continued to claim that slavery was actually an eleemosynary, a charitable, institution because those who laboured under it were better off doing so in America than leading the lives they had led in their former African homeland.

The pope, however, could only offer moral support and could attempt to induce the Catholics in the North to rebel against the Union. They did not. The Southern Catholics remained loyal to the Confederacy and the Northern Catholics remained loyal to the Union.

Matters of morals did not concern Napoleon III. He was interested only in conquest and glory. That was the purpose behind all of his wars. He did not go to battle over economic or cultural or political issues. His only goal was power and glory.

He planned to attack the United States. Now he would have to do it alone. The only thing preventing him from doing so in 1863 was the tenacious Mexican army which was holding onto its own provisional government.

President Lincoln dispatched the most able arbiter for this particular situation - General James Watson Webb - to the court of Napoleon III in 1863 to demand that the Monroe Doctrine be respected and that French troops be removed from Mexico. This was the same General Webb who had visited Napoleon III in New York in 1836 while Louis was in exile in the United States. That's why Lincoln gave this assignment to Webb rather than Secretary of State Seward.

Many sources claim that it was Seward who was behind the meeting with Napoleon III, not realizing the reality of the situation because of politics. The Union government preferred that it appear that the Secretary of State was behind the measure to force Napoleon out of Mexico and not Webb. Even the man who implemented the order – General Sheridan – considered the order as coming from Seward.

The only response from Napoleon III of any substance at this time was, ". . . at all events, my intention is to withdraw as soon as honour and the interest that I am now engaged allow me." He added that he hoped that the United States would not attempt to expel him by force because that would cause him to "change all my plans."

Napoleon III refused to remove his troops. More than that, he installed his own ruler in Mexico - Maximilian.

President Lincoln could do nothing at this time to remove the French threat. It isn't clear why the Emperor simply did not sign a treaty with the Confederacy and attack the Union. It is almost as if there were a divine presence preventing this from happening.

## LINCOLN DEFIES THE EMPEROR

The Confederacy was being soundly beaten, and the other European countries beside France had relinquished plans for invading America. The Emperor would have to send in his army alone to takeover America.

Everything came down to this event. The Army of France was poised on the northern border of Mexico, facing the Union Army under Philip Sheridan. It seemed strangely like a $19^{th}$ century version of the Cuban Missile Crisis with the Russians in 1962.

Once the War Between the States had ended, the Union was prepared to immediately act on removing the threat of Napoleon III from its Southern borders. General Sheridan was ordered to the Mexican border where he faced the French invaders with 50,000 battle-hardened veterans.

President Lincoln was directly confronting the powers of the Emperor. Depart from the borders of our country immediately or you will be forced to do so!

This was the ultimate standoff!

It was a critical time and the gravity of the situation is reflected in the words of General Sheridan who was carrying out the order of the commander in chief of his country. What follows is taken from Sheridan's memoirs as he describes the confrontation with Napoleon III's forces in Mexico, which were being strengthened by ex-Confederates. Note that the Imperialist forces he refers to are the French.

The latter part of June I repaired to Brownsville myself to impress the Imperialists, as much as possible, with the idea that we intended hostilities, and took along my chief of scouts—Major Young—and four of his most trusty men, whom I had had sent from Washington. From Brownsville I despatched all these men to important points in northern Mexico, to glean information regarding the movements of the Imperial forces, and also to gather intelligence about the ex-Confederates who had crossed the Rio Grande. On information furnished by these scouts, I caused General Steele to make demonstrations all along the lower Rio Grande, and at the same time demanded the return of certain munitions of war that had been turned over by ex-Confederates to the Imperial General (Mejia) commanding at Matamoras.

Within the knowledge of my troops, there had gone on formerly the transfer of organized bodies of ex-Confederates to Mexico, in aid of the Imperialists, and at this period it was known that there was in preparation an immigration scheme having in view the colonizing, at Cordova and one or two other places, of all the discontented elements of the defunct Confederacy—Generals Price, Magruder, Maury, and other high personages being promoters of the enterprise, which Maximilian took to readily.

I decided to try again what virtue there might be in a hostile demonstration, and selected the upper Rio Grande for the scene of my attempt. Merritt's cavalry and the Fourth Corps still being at San Antonio, I went to that place and reviewed these troops, and having prepared them with some ostentation for a campaign, of course it was bruited about that we were going to invade Mexico. Then, escorted by a regiment of horse I proceeded hastily to Fort Duncan, on the Rio Grande just opposite the Mexican town of Piedras Negras.

Ample corroboration of the reports then circulated was found in my inquiries regarding the quantity of forage we could depend upon getting in Mexico, our arrangements for its purchase, and my sending a pontoon train to Brownsville, together with which was cited the renewed activity of the troops along the lower Rio Grande. These reports and demonstrations resulted in alarming the Imperialists so much that they withdrew the French and Austrian soldiers from Matamoras, and practically abandoned the whole of northern Mexico as far down as Monterey, with the exception of Matamoras, where General Mejia continued to hang on with a garrison of renegade Mexicans.

And, finally, Napoleon III realized that he would not be allowed to remain in Mexico, and the despot issued the following order:

"To GENERAL CASTELNAU, at Mexico.

"Received your despatch of the 9th December. Do not compel the Emperor to abdicate, but do not delay the departure of the troops; bring back all those who will not remain there.

"NAPOLEON."

General Juarez of the Mexican National Forces did not waste any time attacking the troops that were loyal to Archduke Maximilian and he regained control of Mexico City.

Sadly, Emperor Maximilian was sentenced to be executed. He was not an evil man, but he had come under the power of Napoleon III. Maximilian adopted Mexico as his country, spoke the language fluently, and was on good terms with the public.

Despite pleas for clemency from the rest of the world, his execution was carried out.

His final words:

"I forgive everyone, and I ask everyone to forgive me. May my blood which is about to be shed, be for the good of the country. Viva Mexico, viva la independencia!" (2)

Mexico was no longer a threat to the United States. The Emperor had been vanquished in the Americas.

Lincoln's job was done. He'd saved the Union, eradicated slavery not from just America but from the world, and had defeated the powers of the Emperor.

## LINCOLN ASSASSINATED

The president's own sad end occurred with suddenness. On April 14, 1865 he was shot by John Wilkes Booth in Ford's Theatre. Several hours later the 16th president of the United States was taken from the world.

Harkening back to the final visit Lincoln had had with a group of spiritualists in the White House it is important to note how the meeting concluded. In its way, it was a prognostication of what was to come. Once again borrowing from the book *Was Abraham Lincoln a Spiritualist* this is a description of their parting:

"… you are to be inaugurated the second time." He nodded his head and I continued, "But they also re-affirm that the shadow they have spoken of still hangs over you. He turned half impatiently away and said, "Yes, I know. I have letters from all over the country from your kind of people -mediums, warning me against some dreadful plot against my life. But I don't think the knife is made, or the bullet run, that will reach it. Besides, nobody wants to harm me." A feeling of sadness that I could not conceal nor account for came over me and I said, "Therein lies your danger, Mr. President - your over-confidence in your fellow men."

The old melancholy look that had of late seemed lifted from his face now fell over it, and he said in his subdued, quiet way, "Well, Miss Nettie, I shall live till my work is done, and no earthly power can prevent it. And then it doesn't matter so that I am ready-and that I ever mean to be." Brightening again, he extended a hand to each of us, saying, "Well, I suppose I must bid you good-bye, but we shall hope to see you back again next fall."

"We shall certainly come," we replied, *"if you are here,"* without thinking of the doubts our words implied. "It looks like it now," he answered, and walking with us to a side door, with another cordial shake of the hand, we passed out of his presence the last time. Never again would we meet his welcome smile.

Lincoln himself had many premonitions of his end. However one of them was particularly accurate when taking into account that when he was assassinated he was seated in an upper box seat in Ford's Theatre - a high place.

Mr. Lincoln for years had a presentiment that he would reach a high place and then be stricken down in some tragic way. He took no precautions to keep out of the way of danger.(6)

## FROM EVIL DELIVERED

The following point must be clearly understood. Just as Louis Napoleon had gained his powers with the abdication of King Louis Philippe, so did he then lose all his powers upon the death of Abraham Lincoln.

Now that his opposite in the world was gone, Louis Napoleon could no longer maintain the personage of Emperor. The focus of evil, Louis Napoleon, needed the focus of goodness, Abraham Lincoln, to survive. This idea again refers back to the concept of the balancing counterparts of good and evil described in Thessalonians and other sacred writings.

It cannot be denied that from the time of Lincoln's passing Louis Napoleon returned to the blundering fool he had been prior to gaining his remarkable powers. This isn't a theory; it's fact written in history. Notice the total change in fortunes of Louis Napoleon after Lincoln's assassination.

The Emperor had lost his battle for the New World. Napoleon III was forced to withdraw his troops from the northern border of Mexico and embarked on a graduated removal of his entire army. His long decline into obscurity had begun.

Napoleon III had ruled Europe and most of the world between 1848 and 1864. With the death of Lincoln the world had become a vastly different place. The Emperor had been defeated and would assume a background role in the affairs of the world until his own death.

The European States were following a course of forming into true nations. Italy had become unified with the annexation of former kingdoms like Piedmont. Hungary found its identity. The three great Teutonic countries of Prussia, Austria and Southern Germany were being formed into a unified state by the machinations of Bismarck.

Prussia fought three wars within a six year span, defeating Denmark in 1864, Austria in 1866 and France in 1870. Napoleon III had been duped into remaining neutral in the war between Prussia and Denmark and the war with Austria and had been tricked into taking part in one the most hopeless undertakings in history - the Franco-Prussian War.

What this implies is that Louis Napoleon was once again the buffoon. The same buffoon he had been prior to Louis Philippe's ouster from the throne of France in 1848. It was as stark and as sudden as that. One moment he was deciding the history of

Europe and the world, and the next moment he was bumbling from one disaster to another.

One by one all of the gains that Napoleon III had made across the world were taken from him either by a country forming into a nation with a single identity rather than a mere conglomeration of states or by the possession in question simply breaking its ties with France.

The ill-advised Franco-Prussian War brought a final end to the reign of Napoleon III. Prince Edward Otto Leopold von Bismarck of Prussia sought to unify the Germanic States and eradicate French power. He connived and deceived to instigate the war and once the war was begun he annihilated France.

The Franco-Prussian War was a purely political creation. The throne of Spain had been left vacant due to the Revolution of 1868 and Bismarck named Leopold, prince of Hohenzollern-Sigmaringen, to rule in that country. This incensed Napoleon III because he did not want to see a Spanish-Prussian alliance formed. So, Louis would throw a tantrum – back to his old self.

When France strongly objected, the candidacy of Prince Leopold was withdrawn. Napoleon III wanted more than that. He wanted to be assured that the candidacy would never again be offered to Prince Leopold. And he wanted still even more than that. He demanded an official apology in writing from William I, King of Prussia!

What he got instead was an intricately worded dispatch which was altered just enough to anger both France and Southern Germany and bring about one of the most pointless wars ever fought!

On July 19, 1870 France declared war on Prussia. The Southern German States joined their Germanic allies and waged war against France. The army of France was greatly depleted and a large portion of it was still in the New World, very slowly returning to Europe per the agreement with the United States. The army simply did not have the resources to return home to France!

Both Prussia and their allies were well prepared for war at this time and put a much larger and better equipped army in the field than France could come close to mustering. The result was defeat after defeat for France until the final battle at Sedan on September 1, 1870 when Napoleon III surrendered.

Louis Napoleon and his entire army were made prisoners and then rebellion broke out in France. The empire ended and the Third Republic was proclaimed. The German army held Paris under siege and on January 28, 1781 the new government in Paris also surrendered to the Germans. Alsace and Lorraine were seceded to the Germans at this time and huge reparations were demanded. France was occupied by Germany until these were paid.

A defeated Louis Napoleon returned to Camden Place at Chislehurst, Kent, England. Here he spent his last miserable days in the same house that was purchased for him for this occasion thirty years before by a psychic admirer of his.

Louis Napoleon died on January 9, 1873 during a lengthy medical process to break up a bladder stone. The official cause of death was kidney failure and septicemia.

Despite all of his claims to be a champion of the people, very few of his actions did anything to better the lives of any citizen of France. In the end he impoverished the country due to his incessant chase after personal glory. His rule could best be described as one of universal cruelty and misery.

The great Victor Hugo most accurately summarized the legacy of Napoleon III:

> The workman in rags, with naked feet, to whom the summer brings no bread and the winter no wood, whose aged mother lies languishing upon a foul straw mattress, whose young daughter prostitutes herself at the corners of the streets to live, whose little children shiver with hunger, fever, and cold, in the paltry lodging-houses of the Faubourg Saint-Marceau, in the garrets of Rouen, in the cellars of Lisle, do they think of him? What becomes of him? What do they do for him? Die, dog! (4)

Harsh words? Maybe not so harsh when remembering that Napoleon III accepted the following report with pleasure and satisfaction during his days of ruthless power:

> "Our infantry has massacred the defenders of the place to the last man; the cavalry sabred all who attempted to flee. Not one of these fanatics has escaped us. I do not know what has become of the Sherriff, but he will be found." He was found among the dead. (1)

## OTHER LEGACIES

What of Abraham Lincoln? His honesty and decency are well known and do not need any additional proclamations. His own words best describe the legacy that Abraham Lincoln left to the world:

> With malice toward none, with charity for all, with firmness in the right as God has given us to see the right, let us strive on to finish the work we are in, to bind the nation's wounds, to care for him who shall have borne the battle and for his widow and orphan, to do all which may achieve and cherish a just and lasting peace among ourselves and with all nations. (Lincoln speech)

What became of Pope Pius IX? In 1870 a popular revolution swept Italy and all of the Papal States were lost. The pope locked himself in the Vatican where he remained a self-imposed prisoner for the rest of his life. He died in 1878.

Pope Pius IX would best be remembered by one of his own statements released in his syllabus of errors:

39. The State, as being the origin and source of all rights, is endowed with a certain right not circumscribed by any limits. -- Allocution "Maxima quidem," June 9, 1862.

In other words, the state is all powerful and civil liberties are illusions.

These would be the three individuals' verbal epitaphs. The final physical disposition of each man is actually the best testament of how each would be viewed by posterity.

Pope Pius IX was so hated by the people of his country that they attempted to break up his funeral procession and throw his coffin into the Tiber River.

Napoleon III died alone and un-mourned in exile in England after dying from a mishandled medical procedure.

Over 30 million adoring people paid their respects to President Lincoln along a 1,700 mile long train trip to his final destination in Springfield, Illinois.

# CONCLUSION

It has been clearly demonstrated that Napoleon III and Abraham Lincoln existed at the two poles of good and evil in the world of the early and mid 19th century.

Two critical events occurred to show when Lincoln and Napoleon III assumed their positions of greatness. The first occurred in 1848 when King Louis Philippe abdicated the French throne. Simultaneously with this event the previously buffoon-like character of Louis Napoleon was seemingly satanically changed to that of a self-possessed highly organized individual who had the ability to conquer the world.

This is a fact demonstrated by the actions taken by Napoleon III. Before this date he was a bumbling fool who attempted to takeover the government of France by waging a one-man attack on an army garrison in Strasbourg and then again in Boulogne. After the date of King Louis Philippe's abdication Louis Napoleon successfully ran for president of France, arranged a coup which made him dictator and then set the stage for his declaring himself emperor.

The second major event that critically impacted on the world was the assassination of Abraham Lincoln. Lincoln had succeeded in his mission on earth and had countered the evil force of the Emperor. The primary way he did this was by destroying slavery at its foundation. The effects of this were felt worldwide. Once Lincoln was no longer on this earth his evil counterpart could no longer function as an Emperor.

Louis Napoleon resumed his former character as a bumbling fool. The proof is historically factual. In the late 1860's Napoleon III lost hold of all the gains he had won throughout Europe and the world as must happen with all such ill-gotten gains. His army was ejected from the New World. And finally he was duped by Otto Bismarck to declare a completely nonsensical war on Prussia, a war that France could not possibly have won. A main portion of the army of France was still en route from the New World.

These are facts and they clearly correspond to the change in Napoleon III's demeanor upon the abdication of Louis Philippe and the death of Lincoln. They correspond precisely.

Abraham Lincoln's legacy was to eradicate slavery from the world, not just the United States. Once he finally realized that in order to end the War Between the States he must end slavery forever by issuing the Emancipation Proclamation history changed.

All consideration of negotiating an armistice with the Confederacy was forever abandoned by the European powers which had been seeking a way to overpower the United States. Napoleon III's dream of vanquishing the Union and allowing slavery to exist in the North American Continent for the foreseeable future was destroyed.

Similarly, the monarchies of the world which had hoped to maintain their form of slavery over their downtrodden subjects had to relinquish this desire due to the new concept of universal freedom spreading across the globe, initiated by Lincoln's actions.

Had Napoleon III truly sold himself to the Devil as one of the clerics at the Vatican hold told the pope? As wildly farfetched as this seems, there appears to be a possibility of truth in this statement at least on a philosophical level.

He did have one highly enigmatic benefactor, however, who seemed to have unusual powers. have one This was the man known only as Major Frazer. He was a man of infinite intelligence who seemed to be an expert on all subjects. Frazer was a man who came and went from locations with the speed of a lightning flash yet was always in the background like a knowledgeable shadow. No one knew who he was or where he came from. His description would seem to be a perfect match for that of Satan abroad on the earth. But even he seemed to vanish in the presence of Abraham Lincoln.

**THE END**

# APPENDIX - A.T. STEWART

This treatise has been filled with anomalies and bizarre coincidences. One of the most bizarre, however, is something that A.T. Stewart, Abraham Lincoln, and Napoleon III share in common. In 1836 while on a tour of the United States Napoleon III was entertained by the wealthy financier A. T. Stewart in his grand mansion.

Abraham Lincoln never met either man in person, but he does share one very important thing in common with A. T. Stewart. Both men were the object of posthumous kidnapping attempts!

On November 7, 1876 the body of Abraham Lincoln was nearly kidnapped from his tomb in Springfield, Illinois. The plan was to hold the body for ransom. Some believe that the plot was foiled. Many others don't.

However, a few months later the same fate befell the corpse of A. T. Stewart. He too was kidnapped from his tomb and held for ransom. The outcome was different in his case. A ransom of $20,000 was paid for the corpse, but the body was never returned.

How ironic is it that in a strange kind of way these three men knew one another?

> In New York Prince Louis stopped at Washington Hall, a hotel built in 1810, which occupied about half the block on the east side of Broadway between Chambers and Reade Streets. The building was then one of the finest in the city. There were no club houses in New York at that early day, and the celbrated "Bread and Cheese Club" founded by James Fenimore Cooper in 1824 met there. One of the houses on the same block contained two stores about twelve feet wide, one of which was occupied by A. T. Stewart. In 1844, Stewart bought Washington Hall, and on the site, which was finally extended so as to include the entire block front, he erected a fine marble building for his store. When he moved up to Tenth Street in 1862, the store was turned into an office building. It is now owned by Frank A. Munsey and occupied by "The Sun and New York Herald." (2)

The *New York Times* ran a story in 1877 about a potential heir to the A.T. Stewart estate.

## ANOTHER STEWART CLAIMANT

On Monday night, a well-dressed man named Milton Church,who recently arrived in this city from Europe, called atthe residence of Mrs. A.T. Stewart, in Thirty-Fourth Street, near Fifth Avenue, and told the servant who waited upon him that he was Mrs. Stewart's son, and had come tovisit her as he had not seen her since he was kidnappedabout 28 years ago. The servant informed him that he mustbe mistaken, but he still persisted and finally becameso troublesome that he was handed over to a policeman. The prisoner was arraigned before Justice Otterbourgyesterday at the Second District Police Court where it was apparent to the Justice that the unfortunate man was insane. The prisoner was committed to the care of the Commissioners of Charities and Correction.

# REFERENCES

*Intimate Memoirs of Napoleon III*
By Baron D'Ambes
Stanley Paul & Company
London 1880        (1)


*Napoleon the Third - The Romance of an Emperor*
By Walter Geer
Jonathan Cape
London 1921        (2)


*Napoleon the Little*
By Victor Hugo
Sheldon & Company
New York City 1870        (3)


*The Life of Napoleon III*
By Archibald Forbes
Longmans, Green & Co.
London 1880        (4)

*Abraham Lincoln the True story of a Great Life*
By William Herndon & Jesse Weik
D. Appleton And Company
New York and London         (5)


Many items concerning Lincoln were taken from his listing of daily logs.

Other references:

*The last Days of papal Rome*
By Raffaele DeCesare
Archibald Constable & Co.    1909

## NAPOLEON III AS EMPEROR

*The Great Tribulation; or, Things Coming on The Earth*
By John Cumming
Rudd & Carleton  1860

*The European Sphinx; or, Satan's Masterpiece*
Clinton Colegrove
Buffalo, NY 1866

*The Last Times and the Great Consummation*
By Joseph Augustus Seiss
Blakeman & Mason
New York City 1863


*Destined Monarch of The world*
By Mrs. Sarah P. Walsworth
Self publication
Rochester, NY 1894 (6)


CONFRONTING NAPOLEON III IN MEXICO


*Memoirs of General Sheridan*
Volume II. Part 5
Philip Henry Sheridan

ZCZVZVZ

ZVZBZZC

www.ingramcontent.com/pod-product-compliance
Lightning Source LLC
Chambersburg PA
CBHW020110020526
44112CB00033B/1168